CHAU

THE KNIGH

AND

THE CLERK ᴜ ɪ ᴀʟᴇ

by
ELIZABETH SALTER

*Professor of Mediaeval English Literature
University of York*

EDWARD ARNOLD (PUBLISHERS) LTD.

41 Maddox Street, London W.1

First published 1962
Reprinted 1965, 1967, 1969

Boards edition SBN: 7131 5060 2

Paper edition SBN: 7131 5061 0

Printed in Great Britain by
Butler & Tanner Ltd., Frome and London

General Preface

It has become increasingly clear in recent years that what both the advanced Sixth Former and the university student need most by way of help in their literary studies are close critical analyses and evaluations of individual works. Generalisations about periods or authors, general chat about the Augustan Age or the Romantic Movement, have their uses; but often they provide merely the illusion of knowledge and understanding of literature. All too often students come up to the university under the impression that what is required of them in their English literature courses is the referring of particular works to the appropriate generalisations about the writer or his period. Without taking up the anti-historical position of some of the American 'New Critics', we can nevertheless recognise the need for critical studies that concentrate on the work of literary art rather than on its historical background or cultural environment.

The present series is therefore designed to provide studies of individual plays, novels and groups of poems and essays, which are known to be widely studied in Sixth Forms and in universities. The emphasis is on clarification and evaluation; biographical and historical facts, while they may, of course, be referred to as helpful to an understanding of particular elements in a writer's work, will be subordinated to critical discussion. What kind of work is this? What exactly goes on here? How good is this work, and why? These are the questions which each writer will try to answer.

Contents

1. Introductory

When Chaucer tells us, at the end of the *General Prologue* to the *Canterbury Tales*, that he will report the matter and manner of the pilgrims with full dramatic verisimilitude—

> But first I pray yow, of youre curteisye,
> That ye n'arrette it nat my vileynye,
> Thogh that I pleynly speke in this mateere,
> To telle yow hir wordes and hir cheere,
> Ne thogh I speke hir wordes properly . . .
> Whoso shal telle a tale after a man,
> He moot reherce, as ny as evere he kan
> Everich a word . . .
> Or ellis he moot telle his tale untrewe . . .
>
> (*Gen. Prol.*, 725 foll.[1])

he raises certain expectations which, in the case of many of the *Tales*, he has only a limited intention of fulfilling. The relationship of pilgrim and tale is often complex—sometimes even enigmatic. No amount of ingenious argument can conceal the fact that in practice, if not in theory, Chaucer's narrative techniques are very rarely concerned with fidelity to the nature and capabilities of the character who tells the tale. The *Miller's* and the *Merchant's Tales* are obvious examples: the one remarkable for an understanding of pace and precise timing in humorous narrative, the other for a calculated display of human weakness, and *both* quite out of the reach of their 'authors' as they appear in the *General Prologue* and links to the *Tales*. But in the case of the Knight and the Clerk we seem to meet, initially, at least, fewer difficulties. They are first presented to us in a highly idealised, conventionalised way; they are 'pure' portraits of men whose qualities are entirely admirable. Chaucer feels no need, when dealing with them, as opposed to some of their companions, to make use of the innuendo, the deliberately incongruous detail, the disclaimer of damaging intent which only serves to stress the damage already done. Among the varied sorts of realism we find in the *General Prologue*—pictorial, dramatic, grotesque—figures such as the Knight and Clerk stand

---

[1] All quotations are taken from the *Complete Works* ed. F. N. Robinson (O.U.P., 1957).

out for their clearly conceived function as both people and ideals. They have their living connection with fourteenth-century society: Chaucer is skilful with his circumstantial evidence—the carefully charted career of the Knight, his travel-stained clothes, the Clerk's bed-side reading, his threadbare cloak. But they represent most importantly two different kinds of aspiration. They are beings dedicated to higher service—each in his own way, to God.

From the Knight we might reasonably expect a tale of chivalric idealism, for 'He was a verray, parfit gentil knyght', and from the Clerk a tale 'sownynge in moral vertu . . .' And in many respects—though not, as we shall see, in all—the *Tales* do remind us of the nature of their tellers; like Knight and Clerk, they both move and exalt, they have contemporary and timeless significance. It is not surprising to find that neither Knight nor Clerk chooses a story with natural opportunities for subtle character study, dramatic interplay, or strongly humorous effects. We could perhaps anticipate that if they deal with the theme of human love, they will take a wide perspective upon it, attempting to see it as part of a universal pattern which comprehends human and divine. Then also, these men, who represent two of the most distinctive of mediaeval institutions, learning and chivalry, may be expected to entertain their fellow-pilgrims with works which contain elements uncompromisingly mediaeval. The modern reader who has managed to gain almost direct access to the *Nun's Priest's Tale*, for instance, or to the *Wife of Bath's Prologue*, may easily find himself among unfamiliar conventions of art and thought. Indeed, he may find the general assumptions upon which both *Tales* are based unpalatable.

Yet both have a theme of permanent interest to us; the question they ask, the subject they debate—sometimes with dramatic decorum, in the voice of Knight and Clerk, sometimes with imaginative audacity, in a voice which can only be Chaucer's—is summed up by Arcite of the *Knight's Tale*:

'What is this world? what asketh men to have?' (2777)

And they contain some of Chaucer's finest poetry. In ways which challenge and delight, they show the remarkable diversity of his mature powers—the one as rich with brilliant detail as a tapestry, the other as delicately muted as an alabaster carving.

2. The Knight's Tale

The poem and its source: basic reshaping

Chaucer does not mention the source of the *Knight's Tale* by name, but there is no doubt that he based it upon the *Teseida Delle Nozze D'Emilia*, a 'romantic epic' in twelve books by his contemporary, the Italian Giovanni Boccaccio (1313–75).[1] Boccaccio's work was dedicated to the lady whom he called 'Fiammetta', and is of two-fold nature; epic material, treated 'con bello stilo', is combined with amatory—a combination of heroic and autobiographical elements which is not entirely successful. Beginning on a high note with the martial exploits of Theseus against the Amazons and Creon, it develops into a romantic narrative, much concerned with the psychology of the Palemone-Arcita-Emilia situation. The author's divided aim results in something which is neither epic nor romance, but which is packed with lavish and stately poetry. Chaucer had recognised the wealth of the *Teseida* from the very beginning of his poetic career and had drawn upon it mainly for its decorative, allusive verse and for its complex analysis of a love-dilemma.[2]

But the Italian poem met changing imaginative needs in Chaucer. When he came to make a complete version of the *Teseida* he worked rather differently. The exact history of the translation is not clear, but it seems, from a reference in the *Prologue* to the *Legend of Good Women*, that well before the planning of the *Canterbury Tales* he had finished a poem which told of

> . . . al the love of Palamon and Arcite
> Of Thebes. . . .   (420–1)

We do not know how far this work resembled the *Knight's Tale*: what can be said with certainty is that his dealings with the *Teseida* in the poem we have now to consider, reveal him at the outset as an artist of decisive action. The 9896 lines of the Italian are reduced to 2250; several important passages and many details are added. But no numerical reckoning can give a proper idea of how Chaucer remains deeply indebted to

---

[1] See *Sources and Analogues of Chaucer's Canterbury Tales*, ed. W. F. Bryan and Germaine Dempster (London, 1958), 2nd ed., p. 82 foll.

[2] See R. A. Pratt, 'Chaucer's Use of the *Teseida*', *P.M.L.A.*, LXII (1947).

the *Teseida*—often following lines of Boccaccio's text faithfully—and yet attempts a large-scale recasting of the work. We are bound to admire his firm grasp of the basic problems set by the *Teseida* and his skill in carrying out some essential changes.

Earlier in his career, in the fragmentary poem *Anelida and Arcite*, he had thought it possible to copy the *Teseida's* somewhat incongruous mixture of love motif and epic machinery; by now he has abandoned the attempt. Discarding most of the epic pretensions of the Italian, he treats it, predominantly, as a courtly romance. The basic conflict between two entirely different sorts of material is removed: epic invocations are left out, and the rivalry of the two lovers for their lady is made the central theme. To this end, the first two books of the *Teseida*, telling of Theseus's epic conquests, are compressed into less than 200 lines of the *Knight's Tale*: Arcite's wanderings, after becoming an exile,[1] are similarly rejected, as unnecessary to the main action. The epic catalogue of champions, fighting for Palamon and Arcite in the tournament,[2] is reduced to two splendidly symbolic figures, Lygurge and Emetreus. Even the accounts of fighting, although they keep some of the pseudo-epic similes,[3] move towards the sort of vigorous battle realism mediaeval readers knew well from English romances of the day:

> Out brest the blood with stierne stremes rede;
> With myghty maces the bones they tobreste . . . (2610–11)

All these changes simplify and unify the basic material of the poem.

The minimising of epic elements means, inevitably, some lessening of attention to the character of Theseus, who had played such a large part in the first few books of the *Teseida*. But character generally is strictly subordinated to narrative in the English version. Acting with perfect logic, since the outcome of Boccaccio's story depends upon supernatural, not human, action, Chaucer shows himself far more interested in predicaments than personalities. His lovers, Palamon and Arcite, are distinguishable mainly for their allegiance to differing gods, and the consequences of this—not for their sharply differing characters.

Arcite, who in Boccaccio's work has much more to say than Palamon, and perhaps expresses the poet's own love-sickness for the lady Fiammetta, is approximated much more nearly to his rival in Chaucer's

---

[1] *Teseida*, ed. A. Roncaglia (Bari, 1941), Bk. IV, st. 1 foll.
[2] ibid., Bk. VI, st. 14 foll.
[3] e.g. ll. 1638 foll., 1658, 2626 foll.

version. Even the formal descriptions of the two[1] are omitted. If, in the English, Palamon emerges as a slightly more attractive figure than Arcite, this is due mainly to Chaucer's handling of his fundamental rôle as 'servant of Venus'—a rôle which is allowed to compare favourably with that of Arcite, the 'servant of Mars'. There is, admittedly, some contrast between the ardent lover who prays to Venus

'That if yow list, I shal wel have my love . . .' (2250)

and Arcite who asks directly of Mars

'Yif me the victorie, I aske thee namoore.' (2420)

but it is a contrast which is not developed throughout the poem. Elsewhere he seems anxious to present them in parallel terms, deliberately awarding them similar speeches and actions.[2] The dilemmas in which they find themselves—through little fault of their own—are not used by Chaucer as a means of character study.

Even more marked is his stylisation of the Italian heroine, Emilia. Boccaccio certainly intended her to be an *ideal* representation of all he adored in Fiammetta, who was herself, as he says in his Dedication, a creature 'more celestial than human'. But Emilia has, for all that, some individual features: she is gay as well as beautiful, innocently vain, and she comes to feel deeply about the sufferings of the men who love her. Chaucer's Emelye exists only to provide the immediate cause of the lovers' rivalry. We know little of her feelings and her reactions to the melodramatic scenes in which she is involved; even her physical beauty is conveyed distantly to us, in courtly images.[3] What we *do* know is that she is a prize of inestimable worth: 'up roos the sonne, and up roos Emelye . . .'

In broad outline, Chaucer's adaptation successfully changed what was a mixture of romantic and epic materials into a poem with a unified plot and a consistent, though flat, mode of characterisation. His treatment of the Italian shows in many respects an unmistakable growth of architectonic skill and of self-discipline. Whereas in *Troilus and Criseyde*,[4] for instance, the *Teseida* is still being rifled for 'star' descriptive passages, in the *Knight's Tale* that kind of poetry is enjoyed and utilised, but is made to fulfil definite functions. In *Troilus*, Chaucer draws upon and

[1] *Teseida*, Bk. III, st. 49–50.   [2] See below, pp. 13–14.
[3] ll. 1036–8, for instance, Chaucer's own addition.
[4] Based upon another of Boccaccio's poems, *Il Filostrato*.

develops further the amorous psychology of the two Italian poems; in the *Knight's Tale* he abandons almost completely this 'three-dimensional' way of regarding human beings, and takes a plainer way with character. In certain basic features, the poem which results has much in common with mediaeval romance—a predominant narrative interest, 'typed' character treatment, and a theme combining chivalry and love.

Problems of definition and interpretation

And yet the *Knight's Tale* is not at all a simple poem to define. To describe it as 'remodelled on the lines of a typical chivalric romance' of Chaucer's day would be inadequate. In fact, it makes a far more varied and powerful use of language, is more philosophic and also, perhaps, more enigmatic in the final impression it leaves than any other mediaeval romance. If Chaucer deliberately limits himself in choice of materials and in mode of characterisation, he allows himself great freedom in other directions, and although some of his procedures are designed to simplify, others, not yet considered, create a new kind of complexity.

Style as a guide to meaning

The poem has been likened to a tapestry and to a pageant and it is certainly true that Chaucer's wish to shorten the *Teseida* did not lead him to verbal austerity. Richness and formalism of language are features of the *Knight's Tale* we first notice: elaborate descriptive detail and high rhetorical address play a significantly large part. For in many ways the poem moves as if it were a set of splendid tableaux: the experience of reading it is sometimes similar to that of turning the pages of an illuminated manuscript, in which the life of saint or secular hero is presented as a series of glittering and stylised episodes. But none of these comparisons —tapestry, pageant, manuscript illumination—do proper justice to the variety of styles the *Knight's Tale* contains. This stylistic range is of the greatest interest, since it indicates a range of widely differing themes and attitudes to subject matter: there is no simple generalisation to cover either the whole of the poetry or the total meaning of the *Tale*. One generalisation can be made however about the strongly functional relationship of style and meaning. Even in the more ornate modes of writing, there is no sense of unnecessary luxury. The portraits of Lygurge and Emetreus, for instance,[1] rich as they are in minutiae of physical features, garments, jewels and retinue, and fulfilling no real dramatic

[1] ll. 2128 foll.

need in the story, yet have a vital symbolic significance. For Lygurge fittingly displays the force of Saturn, who, in answer to the plea of his daughter Venus, awards the victory to Palamon. And Emetreus represents the warlike glory of Mars, who sponsors Arcite so powerfully and, as it turns out, so tragically. No detail of their appearance is irrelevant to the conflict being worked out on earthly and heavenly levels: they link human and divine issues emblematically. At the other extreme, the drop into harsh realism of language is not carelessly made, but represents one of the basic themes of the poem—the darkness and suffering which exist at the very centre of this radiant chivalric world.

The language of power and ritual

When we first meet Duke Theseus, he is riding back from his conquest,

> In al his wele, and in his mooste pride ... (895)

and the theme of worldly magnificence is carried throughout the poem by language which stresses the heightened conventions, the almost ritualistic nature of the life led by man in an elevated and aristocratic society. This, and not lack of inventiveness, explains the frequent use of ordered, formulaic speech and theatrical gesture; the appeal to Theseus by the Theban ladies, is appropriately stiff and dignified in its grief:

> 'I, wrecche, which that wepe and wayle thus,
> Was whilom wyf to kyng Cappaneus,
> That starf at Thebes—cursed be that day! ...' (931-3)

and the physical accompaniments—fainting, crying, falling to the ground —are extreme and stylised. So, often, are the initial reactions of the lovers, Palamon and Arcite, to the various strokes of Fortune they have to endure. The poet uses similar emphatic but conventional phraseology to describe Palamon falling in love with Emelye, and Arcite bewailing his exile from Athens: the one cries

> As though he stongen were unto the herte ... (1079)

the other

> The deeth he feeleth thurgh his herte smyte ... (1220)

and their high-set complaints—the one in prison 'everemo' the other free but exiled—are directed along similar lines. Arcite 'wepeth, wayleth, crieth pitously' (l. 1221): Palamon declares 'For I moot wepe and wayle, whil I lyve' (l. 1295). Arcite sees a complete victory for Palamon, and states it with rhetorical paradox:

> 'O deere cosyn Palamon,' quod he,
> 'Thyn is the victorie of this aventure.
> Ful blisfully in prison maistow dure,—
> In prison? certes nay, but in paradys!' (1234-7)

Palamon's view of events is only a variation on the same theme:

> 'Allas,' quod he, 'Arcita, cosyn myn,
> Of al oure strif, God woot, the fruyt is thyn . . .' (1281-2)

This deliberate formalising of language imposes a rhythmical pattern upon the *Tale* which is almost musical in its effect. Repetitive formulas, for instance, work as 'leit-motifs'; Palamon's words

> 'That he was born,' ful ofte he seyde 'allas!' (1073)

come again, with slight change, from Arcite:

> He seyde 'Allas that day that I was born!' . . .
> 'Allas!' quod he, 'that day that I was bore! . . .' (1223 and 1542)

and although they are not in the least dramatic, comment with dignity upon the sad ironies of the narrative. The recurrent use of long-accepted mediaeval metaphors such as fire, wound, and death for the lover's state serves on the one hand to establish quite clearly the type of idealising passion the poem deals with; it serves also as a constant reminder of the violent implications of love. Arcite's insistent references to love and death—

> 'The fresshe beautee sleeth me sodeynly
> Of hire that rometh in the yonder place,
> And but I have hir mercy and hir grace, . . .
> I nam but deed . . .'   (1118-22)

> 'And over al this, to sleen me outrely,
> Love hath his firy dart so brenningly
> Ystiked thurgh my trewe, careful herte,
> That shapen was my deeth erst than my sherte.
> Ye sleen me with youre eyen, Emelye . . .' (1563-7)

have a cumulative power as we move towards the tragic denouement—

> 'Allas, the deeth! allas myn Emelye!' (2773)

And so, indeed, have all the recognisably 'stock' expressions of sudden love, sorrow, or anger as a weapon at the heart;[1] individually they are not particularly impressive, but they build towards and enrich the moments when real weapons threaten life. So when we read

> The brighte swerdes wenten to and fro
> So hidously . . .   (1700–1)

we remember how many internal conflicts have led to this point:

> This Palamoun, that thoughte that thurgh his herte
> He felte a coold swerde sodeynliche glide . . . (1574–5)

The special importance of substance and physical appearance in this aristocratic life is conveyed by wealthy, though controlled, descriptive detail. The funeral rites of Arcite,[2] for instance, give us, at great length and with great visual appeal, a most elaborately devised spectacle of grief. Cloth of gold, white gloves, horses 'that trapped were in steel al glitterynge', harness of 'brend gold', vessels filled with honey, milk, and blood, meticulously listed trees, garlands, myrrh and incense—all these are a fitting gesture of 'richesse' in honour of one who was born 'gentil of condicioun'. The jewels that are cast into the funeral flames seem to symbolise both the material and emotional extravagance of this society. It is, however, a society which has power to limit and order extravagance; just as the mourning ceremonies for Arcite come to a well-defined end (ll. 2967–8) so even the most lavish display of language never gives the impression of mere indulgence. The description of the tournament accumulates vocabulary of strong visual and aural appeal to convey a scene of material splendour:

> Ther maystow seen devisynge of harneys
> So unkouth and so riche, and wroght so weel
> Of goldsmythrye, of browdynge, and of steel;
> The sheeldes brighte, testeres, and trapures,
> Gold-hewen helmes, hauberkes, cote-armures . . .
>   (2496–2500)

But it is crowded, not chaotic. The narrator passes rapidly and logically from one object, activity and person to another, even observing social rank, as he moves from 'lordes in parementz' down to 'yemen on foote and communes many oon'. The violent fighting that follows is

---

[1] e.g. ll. 1079, 1114–18, 1220, 1564–5, 1574–5.
[2] ll. 2853–2966.

sharply realised by imitative sound and a particularly vigorous range
of verbs:

> Ther shyveren shaftes upon sheeldes thikke;
> He feeleth thurgh the herte-spoon the prikke.
> Up spryngen speres twenty foot on highte;
> Out goon the swerdes as the silver brighte;
> The helmes they tohewen and toshrede;
> Out breste the blood with stierne stremes rede . . . (2605–10)

But involvement in the purely physical zest of the battle, the impact
of body and weapon, does not disturb overall artistic patterning. Con-
crete and vivid language is set to deal with a disciplined series of topics.

The description of the three temples built to Theseus's commands
introduces us to an immense show of power manifested in forms of
great beauty and terror. Significantly, they . . . 'coste largely of gold
a fother . . . ', and whatever symbolic references are later to be taken
in, it is clear that, initially, we are meant to be struck with their pal-
pable, visual impressiveness, their 'belle solidité'—carved as they are of
marble, alabaster, coral, and 'walled of stoon'. The details supplied about
'the noble kervyng and the portreitures' (l. 1915) work always towards
a greater sensuous realisation of the object or scene. Though there
were literary sources for the passage, Chaucer's love of the visual
arts—evident over the whole range of his poetry—surely directs the
account of the statue of Venus; aesthetic enjoyment of shape, colour and
gesture is strongly felt in the lines which report how it was

> . . . naked, fletynge in the large see,
> And fro the navele doun al covered was
> With wawes grene, and brighte as any glas.
> A citole in hir righte hand hadde she,
> And on hir heed, ful semely for to se,
> A rose gerland . . .[1]   (1956–61)

In the temple of Mars, substance is oppressively forced upon our
notice: a painted forest, as menacing as any Grünewald landscape, comes

---

[1] In the *Teseida*, Bk. VII, st. 50 foll., Palemone's prayer goes to the
Temple of Venus and sees the goddess herself, naked. Chaucer's description
of the statue takes some details from the *Libellus de Deorum Imaginibus*,
by Albricus Philosophus, and adds others afresh; the 'wawes grene and
brighte as any glas' may have been suggested by an illustration in one
MS. of the *Libellus*.

to sinister life:

> . . . knotty, knarry, bareyne trees olde
> Of stubbes sharpe and hidouse to biholde,
> In which ther ran a rumbel in a swough,
> As though a storm sholde bresten every bough: (1977–80)

The emphatic alliterative style, used also in the account of the tourna-ment,[1] is interesting; this is the nearest Chaucer ever comes to composing in the old alliterative, accentual measure used by his contemporaries of the west and north of England. Poetry of this tradition had long been famous for its descriptive skill in dealing with battle-narrative and rough landscape, and here we may have Chaucer's own acknowledgement of the special evocative power of blocked alliterative vocabulary. But there are less direct means by which a painted temple can be invested with tangible horror. Patterning of hard single consonants, densely clustered consonant groups, and heavy vowel sounds build up a passage of great force and complexity. Such poetry reminds us of the strain of 'iren tough' in Chaucer's imagination:

> The dore was al of adamant eterne,
> Yclenched overthwart and endelong
> With iren tough; and for to make it strong,
> Every pyler, the temple to sustene,
> Was tonne greet, of iren bright and shene. (1990–4)

As we shall see, this massive embodiment of warlike power is no isolated 'set-piece', but a central illustration of one of the most important themes of the poem. In fact the strong relevance of descriptive material to theme is noticeable throughout the *Tale*. These passages just examined express certain values of the society to which Theseus, Palamon and Arcite belong: the store set by brilliant externals, by the translation of the immaterial—pride, joy, fear, grief, animosity—into material ceremonies and rituals. And in their detail, colour, solidity, they give another dimen-sion to the work. What it lacks in depth and subtlety of characterisation, it makes up for in depth and concreteness of setting, and if the figures often seem two-dimensional, the world they inhabit is roundly presented.

The civilisation pictured here in such 'raw and glittering light' is based upon respect for the tangible—the sword, the votive offering, the statue,

---

[1] See above, p. 16.

B

the gold coin. The grief-stricken cry of the Athenian women, on hearing of Arcite's death, need not be intended ironically, but may express an honest though limited value-judgement:

> 'Why woldestow be deed', thise wommen crye,
> 'And haddest gold ynough and Emelye?' (2835–6)

And we can imagine that such an essentially masculine civilisation with its love of pomp, of fighting, its simple though high code of magnanimity, courage, and piety, would be well understood by the 'parfit, gentil knyght' himself. But there are other elements in the world of the *Tale*, some of them disturbing: correspondingly, other styles interleave the descriptive splendour and the stylised oratory we have just been noticing.

The language of concept, criticism, and realism

The philosophic material introduced by Chaucer into his Italian source required language of semi-technical, abstract nature: Chaucer's audience would easily have recognised the Boethian Latin[1] behind dignified speeches such as that of Arcite at the beginning of the story:

> 'Allas, why pleynen folk so in commune
> On purveiaunce of God, or of Fortune . . .' (1251–2)

or that of Duke Theseus, towards the end:

> 'The Firste Moevere of the cause above,
> Whan he first made the faire cheyne of love,
> Greet was th' effect, and heigh was his entente . . .'[2] (2987–90)

Comment upon events is not only made, however, in this specialised stylistic mode. It is true that the characters are not given full realistic treatment, and that they more often soliloquise or address each other with rhetorical words and gestures. But there are occasions when the natural speaking voice comes through, using trenchant, dramatic lan-

[1] Boethius, d. 524. His *De Consolatione Philosophiae* was translated by Chaucer. See Robinson, *Works*, pp. 373–448.

[2] The Boethian passages upon which parts of this speech are based are given conveniently in the edition of the *Knight's Tale* by J. A. W. Bennett (London, 1958), pp. 146–7. They range from Bk. I, metr. 5, Bk. II, metr. 8, Bk. III, metr. 9, to Bk. IV, pr. 6 and metr. 6.

guage, and expressing surprisingly pointed opinions. Arcite's initial summing-up of the love dilemma in which he and Palamon find themselves has a crispness of attack and terminology quite unlike his usual mannered delivery:

> 'And therefore, at the kynges court, my brother,
> Ech man for hymself, ther is noon oother . . .' (1181–2)

Duke Theseus can also find colloquial words for an unexpectedly common-sense, almost jocular, view of the lovers' duel:

> 'A man moot ben a fool, or yong or oold . . .' (1812)

But such language is put to deeper purposes than those of Theseus. For although the poem portrays many aspects of Athenian life with confident exuberance, it also looks intently at the darker implications of divine and human affairs. If we are introduced to warlike violence by the splendid description of the banner of Theseus—

> The rede statue of Mars, with spere and targe,
> So shyneth in his white baner large,
> That alle the feeldes glyteren up and doun . . . (975–7)

we are later refused the comfort of this protective and glamorous language, and made to feel directly the reverse of the matter. The 'glory' of Mars is conveyed quite as truthfully and savagely by his statue in the temple and by the hideous wall-paintings of non-chivalrous death which we find there.[1] Questions are raised about universal order and justice in words of uncomfortable exactness:

> '. . . O crueel goddes that governe
> This world with byndyng of youre worde eterne, . . .
> What is mankynde moore unto you holde
> Than is the sheep that rouketh in the folde? . . .' (1303–4, 1307–8)

And the crowded, excited activities of the tournament are prefaced by Saturn's revelation of disaster in severest, plainest terms:

> 'Myn is the drenchyng in the see so wan;
> Myn is the prison in the derke cote;
> Myn is the stranglyng and hangyng by the throte . . .' (2456–8)

This movement from images of chivalric ritual and attitudes of extravagant emotion to philosophic analysis, humorous deflation, and

[1] See below, pp. 26–7.

pungent, bitter commentary is remarkable on a purely stylistic plane. But we have to consider what this stylistic variety, and, in particular, the dramatic contrast between splendour and harshness, tell us of Chaucer's overall intention in the *Knight's Tale*.

Modes of presentation

Among the many changes which Chaucer worked upon his Italian source, most important for their far-reaching influence are the reflective passages which he gave to the main personages of the *Tale*. Arcite, Palamon and Theseus meditate on death, happiness, providence, turning from personal issues to consider wider metaphysical problems.[1] Arcite's banishment from Athens, Palamon's life-imprisonment, Arcite's death, prompt discussion which restates and then searches to answer the moving question—

'What is this world? what asketh men to have? . . .'

And in so far as this material draws substantially upon the *Consolation of Philosophy*—the central theme of which is the relation of providence to man's happiness—its effect is to increase the 'high seriousness' of the poem. By its positioning and varied emphases, however, it encourages the reader to think more deeply about the nature and implications of the narrative, and about Chaucer's attitude to that sequence of events.

As we have seen, he chose to flatten and stylise the characters of Boccaccio's poem, thus allowing the story itself to stand in bold relief. And as if the story were not sufficiently spectacular, he invites us to weigh its larger significance. By reflective additions to the Italian, he forces our attention to a narrative containing elements of extreme cruelty. These elements are 'high-lighted' from the beginning of the poem onwards. Arcite's reaction to the new-won freedom which is, in fact, a new kind of imprisonment, may be initially theatrical—

He seyde, 'Allas that day that I was born!' (1223)

but it develops into something more sober and impressive. Following Boethian reasoning,[2] he admits that the struggle of man towards 'sovereyne good'[3] is all too often confused and misguided: man, he sees, is

---

[1] In particular, the speeches of Arcite (ll. 1251–72), of Palamon (ll. 1303–33) and of Theseus (ll. 2987–3040).

[2] *Consolation*, Bk. III, pr. 2.   [3] loc. cit.

in some measure responsible for his sufferings:

> 'And to a dronke man the wey is slider.
> And certes, in this world so faren we;
> We seken faste after felicitee,
> But we goon wrong ful often, trewely . . .' (1264-7)

But his submission to the workings of 'God, or of Fortune' stems from
despair rather than from respect: it is useless to fight the Omnipotent and
Incalculable:

> 'And som man wolde out of his prisoun fayn,
> That in his hous is of his meynee slayn.
> Infinite harmes been in this mateere.
> We witen nat what thing we preyen heere . . .
> Syn that I may nat seen you, Emelye,
> I nam but deed; ther nys no remedye . . .' (1257-60, 1273-4)

The sad truth of this will be borne out by his own experience: he who
has already acknowledged his own fallibility and the inexplicable wisdom
of God, will be struck down in the moment of greatest triumph. His
attempts to come to terms with himself and with heavenly 'purveiaunce'
are cruelly rewarded, and he dies questioning, the problem unsolved.

   Palamon's words on the same occasion—Emelye is, for him, visible but
quite inaccessible—move even more strikingly from conventionally
phrased despair—

> Swich sorwe he maketh that the grete tour
> Resouneth of his youlyng and clamour . . . (1277-8)

to a sharp attack upon the arbitrary dispensations of the gods. Some of
the sentiments clearly derive from the complaint of Boethius to God,[1]
and in its original context, this complaint receives brisk correction from
the 'noryce, Philosophie'. In the present context, however, it has an
almost uncanny accuracy and relevance: the gods of the *Tale* are to display exactly those qualities Palamon describes—cruelty, malice, indiffer-
ence. The language he uses is stronger, more incisive than that of the
Boethian lament—

> Thanne seyde he, 'O cruel goddes that governe
> This world with byndyng of youre word eterne,
> And writen in the table of atthamaunt
> Youre parlement and youre eterne graunt,

[1] *Consolation*, Bk. I, metr. 5.

NB

> What is mankynde moore unto you holde
> Than is the sheep that rouketh in the folde? . . .
> What governance is in this prescience,
> That giltelees tormenteth innocence? . . .' (1303–8, 1313–14)

The references to the beast world, though reminiscent of *Ecclesiastes*,[1] stress with greater bitterness and subtlety the helpless condition of man. Constrained in life, he suffers even beyond death:

> 'For slayn is man right as another beest . . .
> And yet encresseth this al my penaunce,
> That man is bounden to his observaunce,
> For Goddes sake, to letten of his wille,
> Ther as a beest may al his lust fulfille.
> And whan a beest is deed, he hath no peyne;
> But man after his deeth moot wepe and pleyne,
> Though in this world he have care and wo . . .' (1309, 1315–20)

For the deities who rule the human condition, Palamon has only fear mingled with contempt:

> 'But I moot be in prisoun thurgh Saturne,
> And eek thurgh Juno, jalous and eek wood,
> That hath destroyed wel ny al the blood
> Of Thebes with his waste walles wyde;
> And Venus sleeth me on that oother syde
> For jalousie and fere of hym Arcite . . .' (1328–33)

Though such accusations may be, in terms of Boethian philosophy, 'benighted',[2] they are most germane to the outcome of this particular story. Palamon's rebellious words will find dramatic justification as the narrative unfolds: the final irony will be reached when he, and not the more orthodox Arcite, is awarded the coveted prize.

NB

The theme of divine callousness, even divine injustice, has been introduced: the questions asked by Palamon and Arcite involve the reader in much more than just the immediate love-problem. It comes, therefore, as somewhat of a surprise when the narrator of the *Tale*—Knight or Chaucer or anonymous 'persona'—comments comfortably, even jovially, upon the woes of the lovers:

> Yow loveres axe I now this questioun,
> Who hath the worse, Arcite or Palamoun? . . .

[1] *Ecclesiastes*, 3.19.

[2] See B. L. Jefferson, *Chaucer and the Consolation of Philosophy of Boethius* (Princeton, 1917), p. 131.

> Now demeth as yow liste, ye that kan,
> For I wol telle forth as I bigan. (1347–8, 1353–4)

The two voices of the poet: divided purposes

We meet, here, a problem which will assume even greater importance later in the poem. By the end of part one, Chaucer has already shown his intention of dealing variously with his material. Consistent, as we have seen, in certain of the procedures he adopts for the *Tale*,[1] he is equally prepared to abandon consistency. In passing so swiftly from powerful expression to comment which is trivial, almost flippant, he seems to be using two voices: one reveals for us the pain latent in the narrative, the other, less sensitive, speaks with imperfect comprehension of that pain. Dramatic verisimilitude, at any rate, is clearly not at stake; if we think back to the original narrator of the *Tale*, the Knight, it is difficult to credit him with the voice of complaint and criticism— although we can, if we wish, imagine that we hear him in the candid, over-simplified appeal to the audience—'Yow loveres axe I now . . .' This refusal to be limited to any one particular mode of presentation will make for a complex poem, rich in local effects, but not necessarily unified or easy to interpret from a global point of view.

Part two reminds us of this in such a small matter as the description of Palamon's continued imprisonment. The narrator first stresses the miserable conditions in which he lives—

> In derknesse and horrible and strong prisoun
> Thise seven yeer hath seten Palamoun
> Forpyned . . .   (1451–3)

and then withdraws from the situation—

> Who koude ryme in Englyssh proprely
> His martirdom? for sothe it am nat I;
> Therefore I passe as lightly as I may. (1459–61)

This would not be remarkable—it can be defined, after all, as a well-known rhetorical device, used frequently by Chaucer—were it not that the English poem deliberately chooses to bring Palamon's suffering to our notice, as the Italian source does not.[2] Again, the two voices—one

---

[1] See above, p. 9 foll.

[2] The *Teseida* says that both knights were comfortably quartered: Bk. II, st. 98–9.

pressing home the 'derknesse' of the story, the other anxious to evade
responsibility for it. It is true, however, that on the whole, this section of
the poem is comparatively straightforward in approach. It gives some
temporary relief from the overpowering sense of pain, of lives clamped
down in unalterable misery. The lovers act to change their situations, and
sublunary events seem to have taken a vigorous and constructive turn.
Arcite's long meditation in the grove gives way to dialogue: Palamon
and Arcite quarrel, fight, are dramatically interrupted by Duke Theseus:

> This duc his courser with his spores smoot,
> And at a stert he was bitwix hem two,
> And pulled out a swerd, and cride, 'Hoo! . . .' (1704-6)

The poetry has often to deal with business-like arrangements: the
preparations for the first duel, Theseus's plans for his tournament. And
the book ends on a note of cheerful anticipation—the knights depart
'with good hope and with herte blithe' (1878).

Warning that such cheerfulness may be under close, even hostile
observation by higher powers is occasionally given. Arcite's lament
speaks of the 'crueltee' of Juno, the fate of Thebes: he is in no doubt
about the 'ire' of the gods—

> Allas, thou felle Mars! allas, Juno!
> Thus hath youre ire oure lynage al fordo . . . (1559-60)

The tyrannical, uncharitable workings of the god of love are twice
referred to[1]—once in a passage which is almost wholly Chaucer's invention. Theseus muses upon the compulsions which have brought Arcite
and Palamon to the verge of death:

> 'And yet hath love, maugree hir eyen two,
> Broght hem hyder bothe for to dye . . .
> Thus hath hir lord, the god of love, ypayed
> Hir wages and hir fees for hir servyse!' (1796-7, 1802-3)

And yet on none of these occasions are we moved to deep pity or
indignation: Arcite turns from accusing the gods to accusing Emelye of
being the cause of his death. The idiom is that of the courtly love-
complaint—the tone half-desperate, half-detached: 'Ye sleen me with
youre eyen, Emelye!' (l. 1567). Theseus begins with serious reflection,
but soon drops into amused cynicism; he invites our tolerance of the

---

[1] ll. 1623 foll., 1785 foll.

antics of mankind, not our compassion for its suffering. His words are chosen carefully to suggest that we should not take these matters too much to heart:

> 'But yet this is the beste *game* of alle,
> That she for whom they han this *jolitee*
> Kan hem therfore as muche thank as me.
> She woot namoore of al this *hoote fare*, *— heated goings on*
> By God, than woot a *cokkow or an hare!* . . .' (1806–10)
> *knows*   *NB*

The robust, even coarse, common-sense of Theseus provides comfortable reading; like the good-temper of the 'narrator', it offsets the unpleasant-ness of much that has already happened, and much that is likely to happen. When Theseus here invokes the gods, he does so impetuously, almost unthinkingly; neither of his references to 'myghty Mars' [1] sound particularly ominous in their immediate context.

And part three opens with the narrator in optimistic mood. His tone, as he introduces us to the temples of Venus, Mars and Diana, is light and companionable:

> I trowe men wolde deme it necligence
> If I foryete to tellen the dispence
> Of Theseus, that gooth so bisily
> To maken up the lystes roially . . . (1881–4)

It would be difficult to anticipate, from these words, the spectacle of violence and unhappiness inside the temples. Chaucer's intentions are now by no means comfortable, whatever he has led us to expect. The account of the temple of Venus, greatly shortened from Boccaccio's version, includes, in spite of this, many *fresh* details of the sorrows of love—

> The broken slepes, and the sikes colde,
> The sacred teeris, and the waymentynge,
> The firy strokes of the desirynge
> That loves servantz in this lyf enduren . . . (1920–3)

and fresh instances of wickedness inspired by love—Medea, Circe. The rapturous sight of Venus 'fletynge in the large see' cannot quite dispel the first impression of constricting sadness:

> Lo, alle thise folk so caught were in hir las,
> Til they for wo ful ofte seyde, 'Allas!' (1951–2)

[1] ll. 1708, 1747: both are Chaucer's own additions.

In fact, the sensuous 'colour' of the passage describing the statue of the goddess gives added point to the sombre tableau which precedes it; the disastrous and beguiling aspects of passionate love are sharply juxtaposed.

The temple of Mars, grim enough in the sources from which Chaucer worked,[1] receives new emphatic treatment: it puts before the reader a scene of terror which is half painted image and half allegorical tableau. The abstract power of the originals is preserved—sometimes considerably increased, as when 'il cieco Peccare' deepens, imaginatively and intellectually, into

> Ther saugh I first the derke ymaginyng
> Of Felonye, and al the compassyng; (1995-6)

But an element of startling realism is also introduced: the sterile and destructive nature of Mars is illustrated with cold, almost clinical exactness of observation. We are made to understand the precarious triumph of war—

> Saw I Conquest, sittynge in greet honour,
> With the sharpe swerd over his heed
> Hangynge by a soutil twynes threed . . . (2028-30)

as well as the invasion of ordinary life by accident and death—

> The shepne brennynge with the blake smoke . . .
> The sleere of hymself yet saugh I ther,—
> His herte-blood hath bathed al his heer; . . .
> The careyne in the busk, with throte ycorve; . . .
> The sowe freten the child right in the cradel;
> The cook yscalded, for al his longe ladel.
> Noght was foryeten by the infortune of Marte:
>   (2000, 2005-6, 2013, 2019-21)

We catch a glimpse of murder—the moment of striking and the ugly sequel:

> The nayl ydryven in the shode a-nyght;
> The colde deeth, with mouth gapyng upright. (2007-8)

And even where the Italian (or Latin) is used, the subject is particularised, brought into clearer focus: allegory leaps to life in 'The smylere with the

---

[1] *Teseida*, Bk. VII, st. 32 foll., and probably also, Boccaccio's ultimate source, Statius, *Thebaid*, Bk. VII, ll. 40 foll.

knyf under the cloke . . .' and 'Contek, with blody knyf and sharp
manace . . .' (ll. 1999, 2003). By comparison, Boccaccio is mild and
diffuse.[1]

The aim of the English rendering seems to be confirmed when we
reach the statue of the god; a terrible climax has been prepared:

> A wolf ther stood biforn hym at his feet
> With eyen rede, and of a man he eet. (2047–8)

Whatever the origin of this last detail,[2] its function in Chaucer's poem
is to impress us with the savage and threatening rôle of Mars: like
all the additions and variations we have been considering, it gives con-
crete form to the 'manasynge of Mars'. In these circumstances it is
difficult to gauge the bland comment which closes the episode; the
narrator leaves the temple in good spirits:

> With soutil pencel depeynted was this storie
> In redoutynge of Mars and of his glorie.
> Now to the temple of Dyane the chaste
> As shortly as I kan, I wol me haste . . . (2049–52)

Nor does he seem dispirited by what he sees in the temple of Diana. The
wall-paintings in this building are wholly Chaucer's invention, and, as
we might by now expect, he gives us subjects illustrating the power of the
goddess and the suffering of human beings. The capricious vengeance of
Diana is the main theme: Callisto, transformed into a bear 'whan that
Diane aggreved was with here . . .', Actaeon devoured by his own
hounds 'for vengeaunce that he saugh Diane al naked . . .', the fateful
hunt of Meleager 'for which Dyane wroghte hym care and wo . . .'
(ll. 2057, 2066, 2072). In front of the goddess lies a woman in agony
of childbirth, calling upon her 'for hir child so longe was unborn'
(l. 2084). The summing-up of the narrator is again curiously out of
key:

> Wel koude he peynten lifly that it wroghte;
> With many a floryn he the hewes boghte. (2087–8)

In its reminder, however, that these are only *painted* terrors—a fact we

[1] *Teseida*, Bk. VII, st. 34.

[2] Editors suggest that it derives from the mediaeval etymology of Mars—
Mavors: 'mares vorans', 'devourer of males'. The *Libellus* (see above, p. 16,
n. 1) says only that the wolf was 'carrying a sheep'.

may easily, and understandably, have forgotten—it leads on naturally to the enthusiastic description of nobility gathering for the tournament. For the moment we are asked to consider only the brave show of arms, the idealism of those who come to fight 'for love and for encrees of chivalrye'. When we are told that 'the grete Emetreus, the kyng of Inde . . . Cam ridynge lyk the god of armes, Mars' (ll. 2156, 2159) we are clearly meant to recall only one aspect of the martial god. Misery, cruelty, death are obscured by magnificence. Similarly, the honour and privilege of fighting for a lady puts out of mind—for the narrator, at least—the sad and sinister warnings of the temple of Venus: the goddess is now 'blisful Citherea benigne—I mene Venus, honurable and digne' (ll. 2215-16).

But such confidence is to be undermined. Like the optimism of the lovers as they sacrifice to their deities and receive favourable 'signs', it is pathetically inadequate. The intervention of Saturn 'to stynten strif and drede' breaks ominously across the scene, and Chaucer's careful exposition of his nature and sphere of influence (for which his sources give no warrant) does nothing to assure us of a happy or a just outcome. This brilliant and menacing speech by the 'fader of pestilence' [1] brings to a head the poem's insistence upon the pitiful state of man and the revengeful attitude of the gods who shape his destiny. If we needed confirmation of the truth of Palamon's early complaint to the 'crueel goddes', we have it here in most powerful form. Whatever the denouement of the story, it is clear, at this point, that it will involve pain and darkness; we realise, with some sense of shock, that the conflict is not so much between Mars and Venus, War and Love, as between two types of violence: Venus will achieve her ends through 'pale Saturnus the colde'; the lovers are to be united through the workings of the god of 'vengeance and pleyn correccioun'. And, as this part of the poem ends on a threatening note, we know that their happiness will be dearly bought.

Part four shows us the cost of happiness with brutal precision. Arcite is fatally wounded not in the glories of the tournament, but in a humiliating accident—we remember Saturn's claim to 'the derke tresons and the castes olde'. Chaucer lays new emphasis upon the physical details, the pain of his delayed death:

> The pipes of his longes gon to swelle,
> And every lacerte in his brest adoun
> Is shent with venym and corrupcioun.

[1] ll. 2453 foll.

> Hym gayneth neither, for to gete his lif,
> Vomyt upward, ne dounward laxatif . . . (2752–6)

And the narrator's brusque summing-up—

> Fare wel phisik! go ber the man to chirche!
> This al and som, that Arcita moot dye . . . (2760–1)

by virtue of its heartlessness points to the waste and pathos of the situation. The last speech of Arcite expresses this waste and pathos in a more directly moving idiom; much shorter than the original, it nevertheless manages to review the bitter sequence of events leading up to this moment. The dying man's baffled and, perhaps, ironic questions

> 'What is this world? what asketh men to have?
> Now with his love, now in his colde grave
> Allone, withouten any compaignye . . .' (2777–9)

replace, poignantly, a whole rhetorical series in the Italian. They remind us of many things: his untried stoicism when first in prison, seeing the hand of Saturn in 'this adversitee' (ll. 1086–8), but not foreseeing it in his death: his trenchant observation as he becomes further experienced in misery—

> 'Infinite harmes been in this mateere.
> We witen nat what thing we preyen heere:' (1259–60)

—an observation which does not, however, prevent him from 'joye and hope wel to fare' (l. 2435) when his prayer to Mars is answered so deceptively with 'Victorie!' It has not been possible for Arcite to learn the full lesson of divine malice; he dies bewildered. But this is a speech of extreme compassion as well as extreme disillusionment. The warm recommendation of Palamon to Emelye—

> 'Foryet nat Palamon, the gentil man . . .' (2797)

contrasts vividly with the calculated actions and words of the deities in the poem. Only those who know at first hand that 'in this world greet pyne is' show any capacity for noble intent or deed; if Arcite does not understand the gods and their 'castes olde', he does now understand a virtue which in this poem is an entirely human prerogative—the virtue of charity.

What follows conforms to the pattern we have already noticed. The dignified closing of Arcite's life is treated with scant ceremony by the narrator himself: he does not know where his soul went 'as I cam nevere', nor does he care to speculate. The man is dead: 'Arcite is coold . . .' He has time for a sly joke at the expense of women[1] before he adjusts his tone and style to describe the scene of grief in Athens. And serious indeed is the comment of 'olde fader Egeus', even if it is familiar in language and sentiment; the commonplace and indisputable theme of 'all must die'—transferred from Theseus's speech in the Italian[2]—is imaged afresh, gracefully and mournfully:

> 'This world nys but a thurghfare ful of wo,
> And we ben pilgrymes passynge to and fro.' (2847–8)

The Chaucerian (and Biblical) touch is admirable—except that the next line, 'Deeth is an ende of every worldly soore', meant as a comfort, recalls an earlier moment in the poem, when Palamon refused the comfort of believing that death brings peace (ll. 1320–1).

Clearly, it is not in the interests of the prescribed happy ending that such thoughts should intrude at this stage. But the words have been spoken, for good or ill. A more determined and comprehensive attempt to give comfort and justify events is made by Theseus after the funeral rites,[3] and here again Arcite's happy deliverance from 'this foule prisoun of this lyf' (l. 3061) is affirmed. The line draws, for its power, upon our realisation (not necessarily shared by Theseus, one feels) that life has in fact been an imprisonment for Arcite: even freedom shut him away from his love. The argument goes further: it makes an appeal for reconciliation based upon man's acceptance of the power, justice and perfection of the divinity which decrees a natural span of life for all things.

Composing a speech which is new in its most striking features,[4] Chaucer works from Boethius[5] to prove the wisdom and all-embracing love of the 'Firste Moevere of the cause above' and the unceasing flow of life out of what is perfect into what is limited and transitory.

The movement towards unification

But with the words of Theseus we have arrived at a decisive stage in

---

[1] ll. 2822–6, Chaucer's addition to the Italian.

[2] *Teseida*, Bk. XII, st. 6.   [3] ll. 2987 foll.

[4] ll. 2987–3016 are entirely new: 3035–8 are expanded out of a mere hint in the Italian, and although the rest of the speech is indebted to the *Teseida*, Bk. XII, st. 6–19, it is in no way a strict translation.

[5] See above, p. 18, n. 2.

the poem. Up to this point, as we have seen, Chaucer has taken a rather variable course in the matter of presentation—often appearing to be in two minds about the significance of his story. While he cannot resist drawing out the less attractive implications of the *Tale*, and inviting his audience to attend closely as he does so, he is equally willing to accept what his sources lay down as acceptable. With a boldness ranging from the blunt to the flippant, he can even be found minimising that same seriousness of attitude which he has been at such pains to induce. But now the narrative nears conclusion, and some general statement has to be made which will allow the audience to approve of the 'blisse and melodye' of the last lines. And it is clear that Chaucer felt the need for synthesis: whether prompted by awareness of the difficulties in his poem or not, he gives the speech of Theseus a far wider philosophical scope than it has in the *Teseida*. Arcite's death is to be seen as yet another proof of the 'wise purveiaunce' of God—or, conceding to the original pagan world of the poem, of 'Juppiter, the kyng'. *Our* difficulty does not lie in reconciling the death of Arcite with a divinely ordained plan, but in reconciling the noble account of this plan with the ugly manifestation of divine motives and activities which Chaucer has allowed his poem to give. Theseus's speech is well positioned, but it is, on analysis, an odd conclusion to a story which has admitted so frankly the lack of dignity, pity or love in the deities who interpret the meaning of 'that same Prince and that Moevere'. While the speech alone could persuade us of some just pattern 'to which the whole creation moves', the preceding poem demonstrates with much feeling that

> As flies to wanton boys, are we to the gods;
> They kill us for their sport.

The narrator, who, over the course of the work, has not shown himself sensitive to finer distinctions, gives no sign now that he is disturbed by Theseus's explanation of divine order and benevolence and the negative proof of it in the lives of mortal subjects. For him, the *Tale* is done; the union of Palamon and Emelye cancels out all memory of what has led to it:

> For now is Palamon in alle wele,
> Lyvynge in blisse, in richesse, and in heele,
> And Emelye hym loveth so tendrely . . . (3101–3)

For the modern reader, the conclusion is not so easy. Neither Theseus's speech nor the cheerful valedictions of the narrator can quite rid the mind of the unanswered question—

> 'What governance is in this prescience,
> That giltelees tormenteth innocence?'

The reasoning of Theseus on the subject of mutability is cogent, but he has nothing to offer as an explanation of why the 'Firste Moevere', 'hym that al may gye', should take such unpleasant ways and employ such unpleasant agents to create 'this foule prisoun of this lyf' (l. 3061) for human beings noble and potential of good.

Artistic balance

The problem is one of balance and emphasis. When we study the use Chaucer made of original materials, there can be no doubt that his imaginative sympathy was called out most strongly by the spectacle of human life subject to cruel and disproportionate strokes of destiny. And, regardless of the dilemma in which he might ultimately find himself, he allowed that sympathy to make strong claims upon him. His portrayal of the sinister gods and their tormented creatures takes in not only the characters and immediate issues of the *Tale* but the whole human condition: we recall the enlarged scope of the paintings in the temple of Mars, and Saturn's cold revelation of limitless power. This portrayal is so memorably done that it becomes very difficult for us to respond uncritically either to a philosophic statement which largely ignores the prominent issue of divine malice or to a happy ending which gives little sign of recognising the unhappiness it builds upon. The reader's predicament is somewhat similar in *The Winter's Tale*: there also a narrative full of extreme and unmotivated cruelty is brought to a 'happy' conclusion, but the reconciliation is hardly sufficient to quieten our uneasiness, even disgust, at the harsh treatment of innocence which makes that reconciliation necessary. Both *The Winter's Tale* and the *Knight's Tale* suggest material for tragedy. This material cannot be fully utilised, however, because of the limiting features of the set narrative structure; while the prescribed story is an inadequate vehicle for the emotions so powerfully expressed by the poetry, it cannot be lightly disposed of.

The meaning of the poem: imaginative license versus narrative coherence

Looking afresh at the *Knight's Tale*, it is important to ask ourselves whether the established view of its meaning—'order, which characterises the structure of the poem, is also the heart of its meaning'[1]—is sufficient. Certainly Chaucer is concerned with pattern: the formal, rhetorical lay-out of the poem has long been recognised—mortal rivalries matched by heavenly, the 'Firste Moevere' matched by Duke Theseus.[2] And, as we have seen, one of Chaucer's directing principles in dealing with the *Teseida* was that of producing a more symmetrical work, even to the point of giving his two heroes similarly phrased speeches. Moreover, life in Athens is shown to be elaborately organised; observance and ritual of all kinds shape experience. But we ought not to confuse rhetorical ordering with imaginative. Chaucer allows the poem to raise imaginative issues which are not resolved by the final philosophic summing-up any more than they are resolved by the bland denouement of the final twenty lines. This is something we have to face in other works of Chaucer. The *Knight's Tale* presents us with it in a particularly urgent form. *Troilus and Criseyde* is an excellent example of a poem which uses a good deal of philosophic and religious material with an eye to *local* richness rather than to overall thematic consistency. Hence, the kind of statement which is intended, in book three, to sanction and hallow the mutual love of Troilus and Criseyde, and so to release the poet's imagination for its immediate task,[3] stands curiously against the overwhelming homiletic censure of the finale:

> Lo here, of payens corsed olde rites . . .
> (Bk. V, 1849 foll.)

But at least, in *Troilus*, we know from the beginning that the human beings of the story will merit some responsibility for the disasters that overtake them. There is a fall from grace, a betrayal, and if it does not justify the all-consuming fierceness of denunciation which Chaucer ultimately steels himself to deliver, it must be judged adversely by a mediaeval Christian poet. And in *Troilus* we are allowed to penetrate the inner lives of the characters so deeply that the tragic course of events seems partially explicable in terms of noble but fallible human nature. In the *Knight's Tale* no similar concession is made: the human beings most painfully involved in the narrative are deliberately envisaged as pawns in

---

[1] C. Muscatine, *Chaucer and the French Tradition* (Berkeley, 1957), p. 181.
[2] D. Everett, *Essays on Middle English Literature* (Oxford, 1955), pp. 168–9.
[3] ll. 12–15, 1746–50, for instance.

C

a game played by the gods—their individuality and freedom of action only apparent when they break through conventional modes of speech and complain with bitterness or despondency about victimisation. The *Tale* confronts us with active malice and passive suffering to an almost unbearable degree: what relief there is—the duel and the plans for a tournament in part two, the tournament itself in part four—also serves to prolong the agony. Chaucer provides for the perceptive reader in the fateful ambiguities of Mercury's words to Arcite—

> . . . 'To Atthenes shaltou wende,
> Ther is thee shapen of thy wo an ende.' (1391–2)

and in Arcite's clear-cut reply—

> 'In hire presence I recche nat to sterve.' (1398)

All the brilliance and noise of the tournament cannot shut out from memory the promise of Saturn to Venus—'I wol thy lust fulfille'.

By choosing to lay stress upon these elements in the story, Chaucer considerably widened his range of emotional and descriptive poetry: by choosing also to encourage reflection, even criticism, he made his task of final and total reconciliation much more complex. We may think that we see, in the strange switches of tone and attitude, in the the 'double voice' of poet-narrator, his half-conscious understanding of this fact: on the one hand, he is impelled to recreate the older story with intelligent scepticism, compassion, dramatic insight—on the other, he is reluctant to admit the significance of what he has done. The imaginative advance and withdrawal of the poem is noticeable throughout. And Theseus's speech is, when examined closely, a withdrawal from rather than a solution of the problem. We may be able to accept the lesson of 'false worldes brotelnesse' from the pitiful wreckage of Troilus's love, but we may question whether the proposition that

> '. . . nature hath nat taken his bigynnyng
> Of no partie or cantel of a thyng,
> But of a thyng that parfit is and stable . . .' (3007–9)

helps us to accept what we have been shown of the sinister dealings of the divine with the human. It is worth considering this speech in some detail, for like the last twenty stanzas of *Troilus and Criseyde*, it moves somewhat arbitrarily among a number of reasons for resignation; its assurance is deceptive, for it relies upon our willingness to put out of mind many of the more uncomfortable aspects of the poem.

Theseus's speech: the crux of the problem

Opening with a substantial Boethian addition to the Italian source, it sets the death of man in its widest context, and not only states the principle of universal mutability but also implies a benevolent providence:

> 'For with that faire cheyne of love he bond
> The fyr, the eyr, the water and the lond
> In certeyn boundes . . .'   (2991–3)

Our comprehension is here invited on the highest philosophic level and in verse of impressive dignity. The eloquence of the passage is beyond doubt: what is debatable is the wisdom of invoking 'the Firste Moevere of the cause above', with its inevitable Christian associations, to cover the activities of Mars, Venus and Saturn in this particular poem. When the succeeding lines (ll. 3017 onwards) draw upon the Italian for their moving images of transitory life—tree, stone, river, man and woman— we cannot help reflecting that Boccaccio gave to Theseus a speech far less ambitious but perhaps more appropriate in the circumstances. A return to Boethian argument (ll. 3035–8) is not sustained; Theseus's reasoning descends to a practical sphere. The injunction

> 'To maken vertu of necessitee,
> And take it weel that we may nat eschue . . .' (3042–3)

represents good sense rather than wisdom: it is not simply wrong but 'folye' to rebel against 'hym that al may gye'. A list of useful points takes the speech further and further away from philosophic matters. We are asked to rejoice that Arcite died 'in his excellence and flour' (l. 3048) and then that he has escaped 'out of this foule prisoun of this lyf' (l. 3061). The backward-looking reference of this last line has already been discussed; only the confident flow of the poetry disguises the basic illogicality of the appeals. The whole affair is put at lowest rating when we are told that grief is useless since Arcite is now beyond gratitude—

> 'Kan he hem thank? Nay, God woot, never a deel . . .' (3084)

The conclusion is brisk—perhaps there is even a note of relief as Theseus bids us to cast-off sorrow and 'thanken Juppiter of al his grace'. If we feel the irony of the phrase as a description of Jupiter's ways, we are quickly led on to other things. The speech, which began in so elevated a manner, passes almost without notice into the narrator's soothing voice as he says goodbye to the story.

It is, surely, a measure of the greatness of Chaucer that his imaginative response to a situation in which innocent creatures confront the wilful use of absolute power was strong enough to disturb the overall balance of his work. As it is, the words of Theseus, 'Why grucchen we, why have we hevynesse . . .', intended as a rallying cry towards cheerful recovery, serve also to emphasise the great gulf which lies between the questions asked by the poet's imagination, and the replies he feels able, in *this* instance, to give.

3. The Clerk's Tale

The poem and its sources

For the Clerk's story of the Marquis Walter and his wife, Griselda, Chaucer relied upon two prose sources—Petrarch's Latin narrative 'de Insigni Obedientia et Fide Uxoris', written between 1373 and 1374, and an undated French version of this, *Le livre Griseldis*.[1] He worked from both throughout the poem, but came gradually to draw more exactly from the French *Livre* which, with its greater simplicity of phrasing and its slight suggestions for a more emotional rendering of the material, suited his purposes well. He made no changes in the general sequence of events, giving what is virtually a paraphrase of his sources. But the *Clerk's Tale* turns out to be very different from either the Latin or the French upon which it is based, and once again we shall find ourselves debating Chaucer's intentions—inquiring what sort of a poem he meant to produce by means of his very significant additions and expansions.

The *Tale* is, in essence, an account of the severe testing of a human being, her emergence, unscathed, from terrible adversity, and her reward for all she has suffered. Probably of a folk tale origin, the story was first told by Boccaccio, at the end of the *Decameron*; though he preserved some of the atmosphere of 'fairy-tale'—the feeling for ritual events, the suspension of disbelief—Boccaccio concentrated his attention upon the Marquis, and made it clear on several occasions that he disapproved strongly of the tyranny of his actions: 'I shall tell you about a Marquess but not of his munificence. It will be about his silly brutality, although good came of it in the end . . .'[2] Twenty years later Petrarch recast Boccaccio's work in a Christian mould, giving the trial a high moral significance which it had not originally possessed. The Marquis becomes more nearly an agent of divine purposes, and Boccaccio's brusque comment 'I do not advise anyone to imitate him' (loc. cit.) is quite out of place. The story now assumes the rôle of an 'exemplum', teaching in the manner of a sermon illustration; a great general lesson about Christian endurance and fidelity is conveyed through a particular, vivid instance of the operation of those virtues.

[1] See *Sources and Analogues*, op. cit., p. 288 foll.
[2] *The Decameron*, tr. R. Aldington (London, 1957), p. 657.

The religious fable: its function and form

Although Chaucer saw the *Clerk's Tale* as part of the dramatic 'marriage-debate' among certain of the Canterbury Pilgrims, he followed both his Latin and French sources by stating, explicitly, that the basic intent of the story is religious:

> This storie is seyd, nat for that wyves sholde
> Folwen Grisilde as in humylitee,
> For it were inportable, though they wolde;
> But for that every wight, in his degree,
> Sholde be constant in adversitee
> As was Grisilde; therefore Petrak writeth
> This storie . . .
> For sith a womman was so pacient
> Unto a mortal man, wel moore us oghte
> Receyven al in gree that God us sent; . . . (1142 foll.)

The central religious function of the fable, as Chaucer inherited it from Petrarch, is stressed in such lines as 'for it were inportable, though they wolde . . .', which delicately remove events from the danger of too close a secular application. However far back in folk lore it began, the *Tale* was received by Chaucer as a kind of parable, and, like parable, it was meant to work partly by bringing divine matters within the range of ordinary human sympathies, and partly by indicating longer, more mysterious perspectives. The use of a human relationship to illuminate a spiritual relationship was well established in purely devotional treatises by Chaucer's time, and English religious writers were practised in managing this somewhat difficult two-way movement between the familiar and the remote: the early thirteenth-century *Ancrene Riwle* (a rule of life for three women recluses) takes something very similar to the skeleton narrative of the *Clerk's Tale* for its section on Temptation; it ensures its success as didactic art by a measure of psychological realism, but also by brevity—we are not long allowed to dwell on the secular aspect, and the story is heavily 'bracketed' by phrases such as '. . . now, observe closely, by an example, how this works . . .' and 'if Jesu Christ . . . acts thus towards you . . .':

> now observe closely, by an example, how this works. When a man has just brought home his (new) wife, he watches her ways tolerantly. Although he may notice in her some traits he doesn't like, he puts up with them, and behaves cheerfully towards her, doing all he can to make her love him deeply, with her whole heart. When he is quite

certain that her love is really fixed upon him, then indeed he feels able to correct her faults openly—faults which previously he endured as if he wasn't aware of them. He becomes very stern, and shows his displeasure in his looks, trying to see whether her love for him can be weakened. At last, when he is convinced that she has been properly trained—that, whatever he does to her, she loves him not less but more and more, if possible, from one day to the next—then he reveals to her that he loves her tenderly, and does all she wants, she whom he loves and knows. Then all that sorrow is turned to joy. If Jesu Christ, your husband, acts thus towards you, do not be surprised . . .[1]

The religious 'application' of the story is briskly made:

. . . in the beginning, it is only courtship, to attract you to love: but as soon as he sees that he is intimately acquainted with you, he will be much more severe with you. But after the trial, in the end, comes great happiness (loc. cit.).

The spiritual context is never really forgotten, and so the motivation of events causes no difficulty. The trial, though artificially intensified by the 'husband', is not senselessly cruel nor long. In any case, the nature of this trial is kept deliberately general—'Whatever he does to her . . .': we are not invited to sympathise with the 'wife' on any specific ground. Since we have known all along that we are seeing the ways of a benevolent creator—his initial condescension into 'marriage' is followed by great forbearance towards human frailty—we can accept wholeheartedly the need for and the fact of human suffering.

If, however, such a story is to be treated at greater length, and outside the limits of a spiritual treatise, the adjustment of religious meaning and secular illustration will be more of a problem. Here now, if the trial is to be bearable—for sufferer and for reader—some inkling of a divine purpose, or at least a divine application, must be given. The deepest meaning of the Griselda 'legend' is contained, so we are told, in the words

> And for oure beste is al his governaunce.
> Lat us thanne lyve in vertuous suffraunce . . . (1161–2)

And we are to understand that it lays down some kind of formula by

[1] Modernised from Part IV of the *Ancrene Riwle*, ed. M. Day (E.E.T.S., O.S. 225, 1952), p. 97. There is a complete translation of the Corpus Christi College, Cambridge, text by M. B. Salu (London, 1955).

which we can learn how to endure the divinely wielded 'sharpe scourges of adversitee' (l. 1157). It does, in fact, amount to a spiritual exercise—Chaucer uses that very word—'as for our exercise' (l. 1156). With this in mind, we can see that the extreme nature of the trial inflicted and the superhuman constancy of purpose in the sufferer can be, if properly managed, important methods of conveying the real significance of this story. If there is anything strange about it from the purely human standpoint, this may be an advantage; we are reading in a genre more nearly comparable to saint's life than to chivalric romance or fabliau. And for such a work to act effectively, some of its language, at least, must strike the eye (and ear) by its special and rare associations—by what one writer has described as the necessary 'oddness' of religious language. The words and phrases used should gradually convince us that 'the situation is only in part perceptual'.[1] Incidents and characters may be invested with strong life, but this will not be simply in the interests of dramatic realism: they will serve something more elevated—something which 'demand(s) the word "God"' (ibid., p. 151). Petrarch's Latin text fulfils these self-imposed conditions well; it disciplines itself for a specifically religious task, resisting the temptation to sentimentalise the story, and imposing a dignified stylisation upon characters, their words and deeds, which directs our responses into the proper devotional channels. The Marquis Walter's opening speech has nothing of the arrogant, menacing quality of its equivalent in Boccaccio; overt religious references

'. . . whatever is good in a man comes not from another, but from God. As I entrust to Him all my welfare, so would I entrust to Him the outcome of my marriage . . .'[2]

indicate, at once, a sphere of activity in which reasons and reconciliation for obscure cruelties may perhaps be found. Walter, himself, whose behaviour is undeniably 'odd' and illogical if we judge it by ordinary human standards of intelligence and compassion, is kept practically uncharacterised. References to his conduct in terms of mundane realism are brief—his desire to try his wife was 'more strange than laudable', a 'harsh caprice' (ibid., pp. 299, 304). But the very persistence and severity of his course assumes a kind of authority as the story moves forward. He has, in fact, the authority of a symbol—he stands for the means by which Griselda may be proved perfect: in Petrarch's version, the justice or

[1] I. T. Ramsey, *Religious Language* (London, 1957), p. 147.
[2] Tr. R. D. French, *A Chaucer Handbook* (New York, 1947), p. 293.

injustice of his actions seems less and less relevant for debate. His uncompromising demands and statements—

'I have tested my wife, not condemned her; I have hidden my
children, not destroyed them' (ibid., p. 310)

dispel ordinary criticism. The concise structure and ordered rhythms of
the Latin seem unchallengeable.[1] We are reminded of the Biblical
injunction—

if thou wilt be perfect . . . come and follow me.[2]

For the trials imposed by Walter are upon a creature already proved
virtuous; like the young man in the Biblical episode, her life is free of
active sin, and full of active good; she too, has no need to be taught
'honour thy father'. Her further suffering *can* be seen as an advanced
stage in the progress towards perfection—a progress traditionally austere
and painful. She is, indeed, required to give up all she has, and respond
to a difficult challenge. Petrarch's rendering of the story relies a good deal
upon an important mediaeval assumption—that the ways of God often
seem harsh and inexplicable to the limited understanding of his creatures,
and that his comfort for human deprivation will be satisfying spiritually,
not materially. Griselda, as Petrarch's dignified conclusion tells us, is a
candidate for highest spiritual commendation—a 'type' or emblem of
constancy.[3]

The French *Livre*, based directly upon Petrarch, keeps this conception
of the legend, on the whole. It gives, however, occasional hints of the
emotional—and not strictly religious—possibilities of the story. When
Griselda is sent back, stripped of all her fine robes, to her poor home, and
her father attempts to cover her in her old gown, it is with difficulty that
he puts it on:

—la couvry a grant mesaise, car la femme estoit devenue grande et
embarnie et la povre robe enrudiee et empiree (*Sources and Analogues,*
p. 323).

Chaucer uses part of this telling detail:

But on her body myghte he it nat brynge,
For rude was the clooth, and moore of age
By dayes fele than at hire mariage. (915-17)

---

[1] See *Sources and Analogues*, p. 328, for instance: 'Sciant qui . . .'
[2] *Matthew*, 19. 21.   [3] See French, op. cit., p. 311.

as he does any detail in Petrarch's Latin which can possibly be interpreted in a pathetic manner. There are comparatively few in the Latin, but it is significant that the comment upon Griselda's state of mind when she hears of Walter's decision to divorce her '. . . tristis, ut puto' (*Sources and Analogues*, p. 318) becomes 'I deme that her herte was ful wo' (l. 753). The French text offers nothing here.

Such proof of a desire to increase pathos raises the whole question of the nature of Chaucer's poem—'What kind of work is this?'

The Tale as religious fable: (i) language and style

There can be no doubt that he well understood the intent of the material he was dealing with; in addition to translating Petrarch's moral application (ll. 1142 foll.) he went to some trouble to increase religious references. Part of the time, certainly, he viewed the *Tale* as a 'mirror for devout souls', and Griselda's trial as a record of purest and highest fortitude. His poetic style seems, on the whole, appropriately disciplined for its task. Simplest, most ordinary language is used—sometimes to provide the kind of social realism we might expect from a work which has a peasant heroine, but more important than this, at key moments and with special sanctions, to give religious overtones. The reader is meant, at times, to be conscious of the poverty and simplicity of the Holy Family or of the extreme humiliation of Christ and his martyrs. On the other hand, a central theme directly concerned with the inner world— intangible bonds, states of mind, and spiritual growth—is enforced by strongly abstract vocabulary. For religious purposes this combination of thoughtfulness and homeliness is excellent. The delicate poise of expression in the following stanza is worth notice: the words—most of which are Chaucer's own addition to the sources—give a satisfactory spiritual analysis of a creature, describe a mortal woman in recognisably human terms '—to hire housbonde evere meke and stable—', and intimate, for the mediaeval reader at least, a likeness to the perfect pattern of humble royalty—the Queen of Heaven:

> No wonder is, for in hire grete estaat
> Hire goost was evere in pleyn humylitee;
> No tendre mouth, noon herte delicaat,
> No pompe, no semblant of roialtee,
> But ful of pacient benyngnytee,
> Discreet and pridelees, ay honurable,
> And to hire housbonde evere meke and stable. (925–31)

While speech is sometimes completely spontaneous and natural

> 'Lat me allone in chesynge of my wyf . . .' (162)
> 'I may nat doon as every plowman may . . .' (799)
> 'Grisilde' quod he, as it were in his pley,
> 'How liketh thee my wyf and hire beautee?' (1030–1)

it is more frequently patterned—not into the rather flamboyant type of stylised rhetoric which we have found occasionally in the *Knight's Tale*, but into moderate formality. Dramatic surprise, the startling word or phrase, have no part in this narrative; the inexorable progress of the trial is well served by language which repeats and accumulates quietly and powerfully. Walter's case for the destruction of his daughter rests upon his desire 'to lyve my lyf with hem [his people] in reste and pees' (l. 487); his words recur on the next ominous occasion—

> 'I wolde lyve in pees, if that I myghte;' (638)

Griselda's first reply '. . . ye mowe save or spille | Youre owene thyng . . .' (ll. 503-4) is echoed by her later:

> 'Ye ben oure lord, dooth with youre owene thyng
> Right as yow list . . .'   (652–3)

The verbal formula, repeated, is an old teaching device—as every mediaeval religious writer knew: here the meeting of temptation by constancy is forcefully described. Similarly, the line ' "This is ynogh, Grisilde myn", quod he', marks out decisively the beginning and end of Griselda's trial: it follows immediately upon her dedication to Walter's purposes—'In werk ne thoght, I nyl yow disobeye . . .' (l. 363)—and comes again after her final proof of 'wyfly stedfastnesse' (l. 1050). A more ironic echo (which will be discussed fully later) can be heard in Griselda's use of Walter's own comfortable words

> 'That day that maked was oure mariage.' (497)

in an exact reference to his changed behaviour:

> '. . . how kynde
> Ye semed by youre speche and youre visage
> The day that maked was oure mariage . . .' (852–4)

The way in which certain words are woven into the fabric of the poem should be noticed. 'Riche' and 'gentil' are obvious examples; they work, in various grammatical forms, over the whole length of the poem, and express a wide number of concepts related to splendour and magnanimity. Not easily defined in any one context, they build up their meaning accumulatively, by usage. Thus the subtle force of 'gentil', when it is spoken for the last time, by Griselda to Walter (l. 852), depends a good deal upon our recollection of how it has threaded its way through the poetry, applied to the inward and outward signs of high and responsible nobility (e.g. ll. 72, 96, 131, 436, 480, 593, etc.). The antithesis at the centre of the poem's theme is stressed by the frequent occurrence of 'riche', 'richely' and 'richesse'. The perfect goodness of Griselda shines austerely against the wordly show of 'grete estaat': even when 'she translated was in swich richesse' (l. 385) her spirit remained simple and pure—'hire goost was evere in pleyn humylitee' (l. 926). And when she is reduced to poverty again, her virtues compensate for the robes in which Walter, as she says, 'richely me cladden' (l. 864).

It is certainly not poverty of invention which drives Chaucer to make constant use of such words. If we examine, for instance, the function of 'litel, povre, pacience, pitous, benigne' in the *Tale*, we can see that they are often set like 'key' words in religious treatises—to carry an insistent message about meaning. In the opening six stanzas of part two, Griselda and her father are introduced to us, and the refrain of 'povre, povrest, povreliche' throughout these stanzas (ll. 200, 204, 205, 213, 222, 232) establishes an emotional pattern which the reader is not likely to forget. Whenever there is reference back to Griselda's origins, the word recurs; the Marquis speaks to her of her former 'povere array', her 'povre estaat' (ll. 467, 473) and he sends for the 'povre Grisildis' (l. 948) to welcome his new bride. At the feast, 'povre array' is once more her lot, and she herself describes her early existence as that of a 'povre fostred creature' (l. 1043). By deliberately limiting his descriptive vocabularly here, Chaucer emphasises the almost symbolic nature of Griselda's poverty; it gains a kind of religious significance.

The same functional importance is given to the word 'pacient', which points clearly to the 'inner' meaning of the fable: used first by Walter when he prepares to assay his wife—'Shewe now youre pacience in youre werkyng' (l. 495)—it comes again at the second and third temptings: 'Beth pacient, and thereof I yow preye' (l. 644), 'And she agayn answerde in pacience' (l. 813). It marks Griselda's return to her father: '. . . dwelleth this flour of wyfly pacience' (l. 919) and concludes the long process of suffering:

And whan this Walter saugh hire pacience (1044)

Closely connected with 'pacient' is 'benigne', which nearly always characterises Griselda's nature and actions. It is she who applies it, on one occasion only, to Walter:

> 'And youre benyngne fader tendrely
> Hath doon yow kept—' (1097-8)

The term is clearly intended to display here all the positive Christian associations it has collected over the poem: it is a verbal climax.

In keeping with the stated aim of the poem, pictorial elements are few. Here is none of the lavish and sensuous description, the driving of attention towards the material texture of life which we have found so often in the *Knight's Tale*. Chaucer even compresses Petrarch's geographical setting of the story—which is not, in itself, particularly realistic —into the briefest of introductions. The language is unspecific and colourless:

> A lusty playn, habundant of vitaille,
> Where many a tour and toun thou mayst biholde . . . (59-60)

Griselda's village is treated summarily, in almost abstract terms; in this Chaucer imitates the restraint of his sources:

> There stood a throop, of site delitable . . . (199 foll.)

We cannot help contrasting, at such a point, the brilliantly circumstantial setting of the *Nun's Priest's Tale*, with its vividly presented '. . . narwe cotage . . . stondyng in a dale . . .' Here, Chaucer refuses to allow the scene to be visualised except in a few strict essentials: the earth, the beasts of labour, the sheep. We are more conscious of activity than countryside: Griselda at work gathering herbs, spinning, cooking, sleeping

> ful hard and nothyng softe— (228)

and fetching water from a well. When we are given a more particular view of her home

> And as she wolde over hir thresshfold gon,
> The markys cam, and gan hire for to calle;
> And she set doun her water pot anon,
> Biside the thresshfold, in an oxes stalle . . . (288-91)

it is on a most significant occasion—Griselda's summons to a new life. Each detail—the threshold, the waterpot, the ox-stall—has been added by Chaucer, and has much more than visual importance. The religious symbolism of the whole passage is strong. Griselda steps over the 'threshold' into a new and hazardous existence: she sets aside the emblem of her peasant life, so full of hard necessity, rigorous simplicity, to enter into a more sumptuous and more taxing world. The ox-stall, which is the immediate background to her momentous act of submission to the Marquis's offer of marriage, shows us the qualities she brings to the approaching trial—charity, humility, a capacity for suffering. The effect is similar to that of many mediaeval Nativity pictures, in which the Holy Family forms a visual and symbolic link between the rough stable with its innocent animals, and the elaborate obeisance of earthly monarchs. But if mediaeval artists let their imaginations run riot in painting the wealth which confronted Mary and the child, Chaucer here keeps his in check. He had conveyed the nature of Griselda's early life by describing the qualities it had developed in her rather than by a harrowing account of the actual physical conditions:

> . . . for she wolde vertu plese,
> She knew wel labour, but noon ydel ese. (216-17)

> . . . in the brest of hir virginitee
> Ther was enclosed rype and sad corage;
> And in greet reverence and charitee
> Hir olde povre fader fostred shee . . . (219-22)

So now, when conveying the nature of her translated state, he limits himself to a few judicious images of luxury which offer very little in the way of strong colour:

> . . . gemmes, set in gold and in asure,
> Brooches and rynges, for Grisildis sake; . . . (254-5)

> Houses of office stuffed with plentee,
> Ther maystow seen, of deyntevous vitaille . . . (264-5)

> A corone on hire heed they han ydressed.
> And sette hire ful of nowches grete and smale (381-2)

The 'hors, snow-whit' upon which Griselda is taken to the palace impresses symbolically rather than visually. With its associations of refinement and delicacy, it points effectively to the transformation which is taking place: in Griselda's former home, there was only an ox-stall. Its purity of colour is appropriately matched to one who is entirely pure of heart. Instead of the glittering ceremony of noble life in the *Knight's Tale*, we find here stress on the duties and responsibilities of nobility:

> . . . in greet lordshipe, if I wel avyse,
> Ther is greet servitude in sondry wyse. (797–8)

Accordingly, the 'revel' at the wedding of Griselda and Walter is summarily passed over, and attention is focused upon the benevolent activity of her 'reign' as Marquise. Vocabulary is predominantly abstract:

> Nat oonly this Griseldis thurgh hir wit
> Koude al the feet of wyfly hoomlinesse,
> But eek, whan that the cas required it,
> The commune profit koude she redresse.
> Ther nas discord, rancour, ne hevynesse
> In al that land, that she ne koude apese . . . (428–33)

as it is also when the Marquis first gives her warning of his terrible desire to try her 'sadnesse': he refers, to her original 'povre estaat, ful lowe' (l. 473), her new 'estaat of heigh noblesse', her 'present dignitee' (ll. 468, 470).

And this remains characteristic of a good deal of the poem. On neither of the occasions when Griselda is faced with the ugly sergeant and her children snatched away, does Chaucer attempt to picture the scene; we are conscious only of words and gestures:

> And to the sergeant mekely she sayde,
> 'Have heer agayn youre litel yonge mayde.' (566–7)

When she walks back to her father's house, we know only that she is 'in her smok, with heed and foot al bare' (l. 895)—a fact which is surely meant to contrast with the splendour of her arrival and to symbolise the extremity of her suffering. Chaucer follows Petrarch and the French source closely in this passage, and allows the strong religious associations to be felt. Griselda's humiliation, her silence, the weeping crowd, recall the final stages in many mediaeval accounts of martyrdoms; in fact they recall verbally the Passion itself:

> . . . but he answered him nothing . . . And there followed him a great company of people, and of women, which also bewailed and lamented him . . . (*Luke*, 23. 9, 27).

> The folk hire folwe, wepynge in hir weye,
> And Fortune ay they cursen as they goon;
> But she fro wepyng kepte hire eyen dreye,
> Ne in this tyme word ne spak she noon . . . (897–900)

Restitution to good fortune is made with the same restraint in descriptive matters. The daughter, travelling back to her parents as a prospective bride, is 'arrayed . . . ful of gemmes clere . . .' (ll. 778-9)—a detail which is, nevertheless, Chaucer's own slight particularisation of the sources.[1] He is, on the whole, unwilling to indulge our visual curiosity about this retinue, and uses vague, colourless terms such as 'fresshe', 'noblesse'; the scene eludes the eye, although the narrative goes forward (ll. 778 foll.)

For Griselda herself, after her triumph, he selects a little discreet detail. She is clad in 'clooth of gold that brighte shoon', and in a '. . . coroune of many a riche stoon . . .' This particularises more than both sources do, and it shows the imaginative decorum of Chaucer: while limiting visual effects, he gives us one vivid glimpse of the woman. Her cloth of gold and crown seem to be the material signs of her transformed—we might almost say, 'transfigured'—state (ll. 1114 foll.).

The Tale as religious fable: (ii) subject matter

As well as these stylistic modulations, there are certain additions to the Latin and French which support a 'spiritual' reading of the *Tale*. Some only temper slightly the unpleasant rôle of the Marquis; others, more significant, strengthen the religious elements in Griselda's speech and actions. So Walter, after his marriage, lives, 'in Goddes pees' (l. 423) not simply 'in pace', or 'en bonne paix'. At the second tempting of Griselda, a new concluding line to his speech

'Beth pacient, and thereof I yow preye.' (644)

gives some dim understanding of a purpose beyond the apparent cruelty of his conduct; so also the religious phrases in his final speech of explanation (ll. 1062 foll.),

'. . . by God, that for us deyde . . . as God my soule save! . . . . . . God forbeede! . . .'

by backward-looking reference, help somewhat to justify events.

Religious associations are increased for Griselda in a more striking way. Chaucer introduces the image of an ox-stall partly to symbolise the lowliness of her origins, and on one occasion to give also a greater visual precision. The first mention of Griselda is prefaced by lines which remind

[1] *Sources and Analogues*, pp. 320, 321.

us of the mystery of the Nativity:

> But hye God somtyme senden kan
> His grace into a litel oxes stalle . . . (206–7)

and, as we have seen, when she receives her call to suffering, she sets down her water-pot 'Biside the threshfold, in an oxes stalle . . .' (l. 291). The same kind of Biblical image is used to characterise the nature of her trial. When her daughter is taken,

> . . . *as a lamb* she sitteth meke and stille,
> And leet this crueel sergeant doon his wille. (538–9)

The likening of Griselda's newly humbled state to that of Job is even more direct:

> Men speke of Job, and moost for his humblesse,
> As clerkes, whan hem list, konne wel endite,
> Namely of men, but as in soothfastnesse. . . .
> Ther kan no man in humblesse hym acquite
> As womman kan . . .   (932–4, 936–7)

Working with these 'historical' religious references to widen and deepen the meaning of Griselda's pain are certain semi-religious references to Fortune. We find her receiving the rumour of Walter's decision to take another wife with philosophic equanimity:

> Disposed was, this humble creature,
> The adversitee of Fortune al t'endure (755–6)

and receiving what may seem to be rather unnecessary advice from Walter himself when he confirms that rumour:

> 'With evene herte I rede yow t'endure
> The strook of Fortune or of aventure.' (811–12)

So far Chaucer's procedures appear to be in accord with those of Petrarch and the French author: if this were all we had to notice about the *Clerk's Tale*, there would be little to say as a summing-up except that here Chaucer admirably drives his poetic energies into a narrow, deep religious channel. We have seen his subtle avoidance of over-familiar realism, of obstructive visual effects, his cultivation of a limited, patterned, echoic language, all in the service of a religious

D

message. This *Tale*, which has been called a 'secular saint's legend', preserves its uncompromising, rigorous nature, as 'ernestful matere' for
part of the time. But what is so interesting is that for the rest of the
time Chaucer works to produce a poem of entirely different aim and
character.

The problem: realism versus symbolism

We have to admit that his most consistent and most dramatic modi-
fications of the Latin and French texts are designed to appeal—in what
is, perhaps, a typically late-mediaeval way—to our sense of 'pathetic
realism'. The *Tale* is constantly pulled in two directions, and, as in the
Knight's Tale, the human sympathies so powerfully evoked by the sight
of unmerited suffering form, ultimately, a barrier to total acceptance
of the work in its original function.

Pathetic realism: Griselda

Noticeable from the very beginning is the very much higher propor-
tion of direct speech the poem contains than either source text. This is not
surprising, when we reflect upon the general tendency of Chaucer's
mature writing to take dramatic shape: in this poem, however, it has the
effect of bringing events into closer focus, and involving the reader more
intimately with Griselda, in particular, as a creature of flesh and blood.
Her thoughts, for instance, when she decides to hurry up with her work
so that she can see the arrival of Walter's chosen bride, are given directly
and in full; the passage is affecting in its innocent enthusiasm:

> '. . . I wole with othere maydens stonde,
> That been my felawes, in oure dore and se
> The markysesse, and therfore wol I fonde
> To doon at hoom, as soone as it may be,
> The labour which that longeth unto me;' (281-5)

But the danger of putting us, so early on, into such close contact with the
inner reasoning of Griselda is clear: the more vividly she emerges as a
sentient being, the less will be her power to move and instruct as a pure
religious symbol. The stanza that follows, with its picture of Griselda
kneeling near the ox-stall, awaiting 'what was the lordes wille', rights the
balance from a devotional point of view; taken together, however, they
illustrate conveniently the double preoccupation of poet or clerkly nar-

rator in this *Tale*—the desire to interpret the story as a human document at the same time as establishing its meaning on a higher spiritual plane.

Humanity constantly asserts itself; there are small, but important additions such as Griselda's final qualifying phrase '. . . though me were looth to deye . . .' (l. 364), when she has already sworn herself 'obedient unto death'. And there are more substantial changes; although, as we have noticed, the scene of the taking of her daughter is left *visually* unspecified, it is given strong emotional 'colour'. Firstly it shows the subtle addition of one pathetic detail; Griselda *begs* the sergeant to let her kiss the child instead of doing so spontaneously:

> And mekely she to the sergeant preyde,
> So as he was a worthy gentil man,
> That she moste kisse hire child er that it deyde . . . (548–50)

The moving juxtaposition of the kiss and death in l. 550 is entirely of Chaucer's making. Secondly, the description of Griselda holding and 'lulling' the child (ll. 551–3) is much fuller than in Petrarch or the French author. And, lastly, there is her address to the child; no basis for this exists in either source. Immediately our compassion is invited:

> And thus she seyde in hire benigne voys,
> 'Fareweel my child! I shal thee nevere see . . .' (554 foll.)

The speech proceeds to take up a point which is mentioned in the sources —the crossing of the child—and to develop it into a pious reminder of another innocent death:

> '. . . I thee have marked with the croys
> Of thilke Fader—blessed moote he be!—
> That for us deyde upon a croys of tre . . .' (556–8)

The passage is a mixture of religious and maternal sentiment; in this it resembles closely the later-mediaeval treatment of Virgin and Child in lyric, meditation, painting and sculpture. Physical love for the child, made practically unbearable by knowledge of its inescapable death—this is the material out of which poets and artists of the fourteenth and fifteenth centuries made a sharp appeal to (what they considered) the hardened heart of man. When Chaucer presses home the human tenderness of Griselda by repeating the word 'litel' ('this litel child', 'youre litel yonge mayde', 'this litel body') in each of the four main stanzas describing the scene, he cannot be accused of an unthinking secularisation of events. Religious echoes would be strong for a mediaeval audience familiar with the rhythms and emotions of lyrics, such as

> I saw a fair maiden
>   Sitten and singe
> Sche lulled a litel child,
>   A swete lording.
> Lullay, mine liking, my dere sone, my sweting . . .[1]

The obedient acceptance of a sorrow in words which really serve to underline the extreme cost of such a sacrifice—

> And to the sergeant mekely she sayde,
>   'Have heer agayn youre litel yonge mayde.' (566–7)

is very similar to Mary's expression of grief over her doomed child. The question we have to ask is whether this kind of religious feeling, once evoked, can help the main purpose of the poem. In the lyrics and the paintings, vivid realisation of human sorrow is usually accompanied by a clear statement about the divine justification for it: good will come of 'temporary' evil, and God's wise plan is recognised, even by those who suffer:

> Lullay, my child, and wepe no more,
> Slepe and now be still.
> The king of bliss thy fader is
> As it was his will.
> (*Early English Lyrics*, p. 119)

And a balancing or supplementing of pathos by some kind of instruction about its larger *meaning* is necessary in this *Tale* too; though we cannot expect such an unequivocal revelation as the lyric gives—'the king of bliss thy fader is'—we must be able to feel that these happenings make proper sense on a higher plane, and that the motive force behind them is not just wilful and therefore unworthy of respect. If Griselda's mother-love is to find more indulgent words than earlier versions of the story allowed, then it is all the more important that Walter's provocation

---

[1] *Early English Lyrics*, ed. E. K. Chambers and F. Sidgwick (London, 1926), p. 131.

should not seem petty and unreasonable in an 'ordinary' human way. We must have some intimation that all this suffering is not basely inflicted; the language of the poem should begin to indicate something special, something mysterious about Walter's actions. This becomes even more necessary as the poem develops and Chaucer admits us further into Griselda's pain. Her humble statement of the very small claims she has upon the children—plain and unemotional in the Latin and French 'neque vero in hijs filijs quicquam habeo preter laborem', 'ne je n'ay riens en ses enffans que l'enffantement' (*Sources and Analogues*, pp. 316, 317) becomes a particularised complaint:

> 'I have noght had no part of children tweyne
> But first siknesse, and after wo and peyne.' (650–1)

Her request to the sergeant, when he takes the second child away, dwells with sad realism on the act to come:

> . . . she preyede hym that, if he myghte,
> Hir litel sone he wolde in erthe grave . . . (680–1)

The effect of 'litel', as on the previous occasion, is to sharpen our realisation of her anguish. Her reply to Walter's announcement of his plan to remarry extracts full emotional value out of the situation. Working closer to the sources at times, Chaucer preserves some feeling of Biblical solemnity:

> 'Naked out of my fadres hous', quod she,
> 'I cam, and naked moot I turne agayn . . .' (871–2)

But the reference to the 'bare womb' halts him, and he develops all its latent, nostalgic sentiment:

> '. . . wherfore I yow preye,
> Lat me nat lyk a worm go by the weye.
> Remembre yow, myn owene lord so deere,
> I was youre wyf, though I unworthy weere.' (879–82)

Even so small a detail as the choice of the word 'leye' in place of the weaker Latin 'fuerunt' or French 'qui a porté' for the line

> '. . . thilke womb in which your children leye . . .' (877)

helps to give the English passage a warmer, more personal tone. And this

is maintained. We have already seen that Chaucer takes care to translate
the French description of Janicula, vainly trying to cover Griselda with
her 'olde coote': as the poem nears its climax, an even greater freedom
of treatment is given to Griselda. She swears to Walter when he requires
the last agonising service of her

> 'Ne nevere, for no wele ne no wo,
> Ne shal the goost withinne myn herte stente
> To love yow best with al my trewe entente.' (971–3)

—a considerable expansion, along sentimental lines, of the brief source
statements, and clearly using the idiom of secular love-lament. It echoes
in Chaucer's own verse: the *Complaint of Venus* (l. 56 etc.) and the *Knight's
Tale* (ll. 2765 foll.). And when she is reunited with her children, the
passion of her words is not muted, but rather accentuated by their
rhetorical casting. Here, now, she reveals all she has hidden behind those
careful non-committal phrases we have learnt to expect of her.

We are allowed to understand the full extent of her suffering not only
by her own words—in which formal apostrophe is so dramatically
adjusted as to seem 'the spontaneous overflow of powerful feelings':

> 'O tendre, o deere, o yonge children myne!
> Youre woful mooder wende stedfastly
> That cruel houndes or som foule vermyne
> Hadde eten yow . . .'   (1093–6)

but also by the unnatural tenacity of her embrace:

> And in hire swough so sadly holdeth she
> Hire children two, whan she gan hem t'embrace,
> That with greet sleighte and greet difficultee
> The children from hire arm they gonne arace. (1100–3)

Both passages are Chaucer's own invention. Significantly, these and the
surrounding stanzas are punctuated by 'pitous, pitously': Chaucer's own
verbal 'key' to the dominant mood is unmistakable—'. . . doun she
falleth | For pitous love . . .', 'pitously wepynge . . .', 'which a pitous
thyng it was to se . . .', 'many a teere on many a pitous face . . .'
(ll. 1079–80, 1082, 1086, 1104). The summing-up of these hours as 'this
pitous day' (l. 1121) must gain our full emotional assent.

But the complete line runs 'Thus hath this pitous daye a blisful ende',
and Chaucer goes on to tell us—here returning to his source-material—
how

> . . . moore solempne in every mannes syght
> This feste was, and gretter of costage
> Than was the revel of hire mariage (1125-7)

The 'blisful ende' reminds us of the central purpose of the poem—to teach clearly about the rewards of perfect patience and fortitude. The reconciliation of Griselda and her family should be acceptable as a victory, and we should certainly be able to sympathise entirely with her when she gives thanks for the preservation of her children:

> '. . . But God, of his mercy,
> And youre benyngne fader tendrely
> Hath doon yow kept . . .' (1096-8)

The possibility of this depends to a great extent upon our view of Walter—the appointed wielder of 'sharpe scourges of adversitee'. Since Chaucer has chosen to depart from his sources at most important moments in the *Tale*, involving himself and his readers in Griselda as a human being and not simply as a religious symbol, we can reasonably expect that he will make some necessary adjustments. Some 'heightening' of Walter's rôle, for instance, an indication that his conduct is to be judged by standards *other* than those of real life would help us to see him, as Griselda does—the high lord and 'benyngne fader'. And there are times when Walter is placed apart; his words to Griselda occasionally hint at greater issues,[1] and Griselda herself attempts to establish his unique position more than once:

> '. . . I woot and wiste alway
> How that betwixen youre magnificence
> And my poverte *no wight kan ne may*
> *Maken comparison* . . .' (814-17)

Dramatic realism: the Marquis

But this is not sufficient to counteract a strong desire to present Walter and his servant in terms of harshest realism. It is a desire which seems to grow as the poem gets under way, and although, as we can see, Chaucer makes sporadic attempts to control it, he cannot rid himself of it. The first two parts of the poem do not give much warning of what may happen; Walter is treated, as we have noticed, straightforwardly, and seriously, in accordance with the sources; one addition even stresses the

[1] See above, p. 48.

'state of grace' he lives in after marriage. But with the opening of part three it begins to be clear that Chaucer, transferring responsibility from the Clerk to himself, is willing to take up and develop further any slightest hint of adverse criticism where Walter is concerned. When the Latin and French texts comment, guardedly, upon Walter's desire to tempt his wife (*Sources and Analogues*, pp. 310, 311) the English text throws caution to the winds, and gives us a passage of fervent indignation:

> . . . what neded it
> Hire for to tempte, and alwey moore and moore,
> Though som men preise it for a subtil wit?
> But as for me, I seye that yvele it sit
> To assaye a wyf whan that it is no nede,
> And putten hire in angwyssh and in drede. (457-62)

Chaucer here commits himself to a line of attack which makes fine dramatic reading, but which cannot help the development of the *Tale* as a moral example. We are predisposed, at this point, to feel the wastefulness of the prolonged testing ('whan that it is no nede') and the pettiness of Walter's motives. It will be more difficult to persuade ourselves of the element of solemn ritual in his actions now that we have been told, in so many words, that what he is about to do is as wicked as it is superfluous— 'yvele it sit'. In the episode that follows, a variety of attitudes emerge: Walter's significant stress upon the need for 'pacience', and Griselda's saint-like submission—'as a lamb she sitteth meke and stille'—argue a controlled religious situation and approach. But Griselda's tender, lingering farewell to the child admits us to a different world, one in which religious and secular modes overlap considerably. The poet's yielding to pathos *has* religious justification as we have seen, but we may suspect that he is taking advantage of such backing to relax control, and elicit human, dramatic responses. The sinister heightening of the sergeant's part in the taking of the child confirms this view: he comes menacingly—'. . . into the chambre he stalked hym ful stille . . .', he seizes the child 'as though he wolde han slayn it er he wente . . .', he is directly characterised as 'crueel', and, indeed, when Griselda begs him to bury the body out of the way of wild beasts, 'he no word wol to that purpos seye' (ll. 525, 536, 539, 573). All these additions, slight individually, give a total impression of deliberate cruelty which greatly increases the pitiable state of Griselda, and blackens, to the same extent, the intentions of Walter. Significantly,

Chaucer rejects both of his sources when he describes Walter's reactions to Griselda's courage: 'vehementer paterna animum pietas movit . . .' and 'il fut meu de grant pitié . . .' (*Sources and Analogues*, pp. 314, 315) become the much colder '. . . *somewhat* this lord hadde routhe in his manere . . .' (l. 579). Moreover, he adds an explanation of Walter's refusal to be swayed by compassion which views the whole matter on a purely secular, despotic plane: '. . . as lordes doon, whan they wol han hir wille . . .' (l. 581).

From then on, the treatment of Walter is predominantly critical. The second tempting is prefaced by a clear condemnation:

> O nedelees was she tempted in assay!
> But wedded men ne knowe no mesure,
> Whan that they fynde a pacient creature. (621–3)

And this casts the light of common-sense upon the next stage of the story. Griselda's noble, collected words to the Marquis

> 'Deth may noght make no comparisoun
> Unto youre love . . .'   (666–7)

and the continued stress on the concept of patience cannot rid the poem of a certain uneasiness. Chaucer's expansions of his source material are often responsible for this: Walter's satisfaction with Griselda's power of endurance reads more like guilty surprise than admiration:

> . . . he caste adoun
> His eyen two, and wondreth that she may
> In pacience suffre al this array;
> And forth he goth with drery contenance,
> But to his herte it was ful greet plesaunce. (668–72)

It is over-explicit in a somewhat fussy way, attempting to 'explain' in terms of psychological truth what the earlier authors realised was incapable of explanation, and left brief, enigmatic: 'admirans femine constanciam, turbato vultu abijt' (*Sources and Analogues*, p. 316). And the comment upon his unslaked desire to test Griselda, which again the sources keep brief, is lengthier and more apologetic. The intimate appeal to the audience—

> But now of wommen wolde I axen fayn,
> If thise assayes myghte nat suffise? (696–7)

(where the Latin has nothing, and the French simply 'je vous prie')
relaxes the tension of the whole passage, and reminds us of the touching,
rather than elevating, scene we have just left. For, once more, Chaucer
has perceptibly changed the atmosphere by his emphasis upon the 'litel
son' Griselda has to lose, the earth and grave, the implacable silence of
the executioner (ll. 681 foll.).

By now there is no doubt in the mind of poet or reader that Walter's
purposes are 'crueel': the word is used advisedly, twice (ll. 734, 740).
Part five of the poem opens, with the uncompromising phrase 'after
his wikke usage', and even though we know that complete reparation
for Griselda's injuries will be made, we are not allowed any increase of
cordiality towards the Marquis. The strongest proof of the irresistible
pull towards human, dramatic values comes in the middle of Griselda's
calm statement of principle (ll. 813 foll.). Here, indeed, the poet
abandons the religious symbol, and gives to Griselda his own melan-
choly, disillusioned interpretation of Walter's behaviour:

> 'O goode God! how gentil and how kynde
> Ye semed by youre speche and youre visage
> The day that maked was oure mariage!
> But sooth is seyd—algate I fynde it trewe,
> For in effect it preeved is on me—
> Love is noght oold as whan that it is newe, . . .' (852–7)

When the only consistent voice of approval turns so critical, it is difficult
not to follow. The rapid swing back to an ideal, religious viewpoint in
the following stanzas, with all their Biblical reminiscences (ll. 871–2,
895 foll.), is the more remarkable. Anxiety to minimise sympathy with
Walter is still apparent, however, in the restrained description of how
he was affected by Griselda's request for 'a smok as I was wont to were',
to cover her body. The Latin and French speak of tears and trembling
—Chaucer barely covers his emotion in general terms:

> But wel unnethes thilke word he spak,
> But wente his way, for routhe and for pitee. (892–4)

When we reach the last stanza of this section—the comparison of
Griselda's trials and virtues to those of Job (ll. 932 foll.)—the dilemma in
which we find ourselves can be defined clearly. The Biblical reference
forces our attention to the divergence between that story and this. The

awesome, mysterious power which permits Job's correction and chasten-ing is presented as beyond question or criticism. If, Job complains, he freely admits his sin:

therefore have uttered that I understood not: things too wonderful for me, which I knew not . . . (*Job*, 42. 3)

Walter, on the other hand, has been so vividly and adversely presented to us, that we are inclined—indeed, encouraged—to believe in his heart-lessness rather than in his inscrutability. And yet his rôle is not envisaged as that of the sanctioned Tempter, Satan, in the *Book of Job*:

And the Lord said unto Satan, Behold, he is in thine hand; but save his life. So went Satan forth from the presence of the Lord and smote Job . . . (*Job*, 2. 6-7)

When Chaucer was led—it seems, irresistibly—to make a character out of Walter, he lost symbolic authority, either for good or for evil: and this authority is exactly what he needs if he is to justify, or to refuse to justify, his apparently wanton acts of cruelty.

By the time we reach the last section of the narrative, Chaucer is not only attacking Walter, but also those of his subjects who approve of his actions:

> Youre doom is fals, your constance yvele preeveth;
> A ful greet fool is he that on yow leeveth.   (1000-1)

The conclusion of the Tale: the reader's dilemma

The speech of explanation (ll. 1051 foll.) is therefore something of a problem. Chaucer adheres to his policy of expanding the source material —with the result that difficulties are expressed more directly rather than resolved. When Walter says

> '. . . I have doon this deede
> For no malice, ne for no crueltee . . .' (1073-4)

he gives form to what has been shaping in our minds. The weak last line

> 'Til I thy purpos knewe and al thy wille.' (1078)

only repeats, more diffusely, what has already been said—'But for

t'assaye in thee thy wommanheede—' and gives an impression of in-
decisiveness, quite absent from the sources. To this, Griselda's passionate
account of her hidden grief comes as fitting climax: it is only hard to
credit fully her definition of Walter's part in events—

> 'And youre *benyngne* fader tendrely
> Hath doon yow kept . . .' (1097–8)

We have not been adequately prepared for that adjective 'benyngne'
as applied to Walter. In a specifically religious context it would have
been possible to accept the rest of her statement—

'—but God, of his mercy, . . . hath doon yow kept . . .' (1096, 1098)

If we could have felt that, in some way, Walter was a worthy agent of
God's desire to 'prove' one of his chosen creatures, then the joy at the
end of the *Tale* would be legitimate—

happy is the man whom God correcteth: therefore despise not thou
the chastening of the Almighty: For he maketh sore, and bindeth up:
he woundeth, and his hands make whole. (*Job*, 5. 17–18)

Griselda's thanks to Walter and to God are moving and perfectly appropriate—as are so many of her utterances throughout the poem—*in
isolation*:

> 'Grauntmercy, lord, God thanke it yow', quod she,
> 'That ye han saved me my children deere!
> Now rekke I nevere to been deed right heere;
> Sith I stonde in youre love and in youre grace,
> No fors of deeth, ne whan my spirit pace! . . .' (1088–92)

The difficulty lies in adjusting them to the predominant Chaucerian
image of Walter—this 'cruel' lord, whose actions are not sufficiently
mysterious and inexplicable to avoid the ordinary human accusation of
malice indulged to the point of luxury. The purity of Griselda's innocent,
submissive words and gestures is contaminated by nearness to this world
of sublunary passions. We are asked to hate, to pity, to judge on her
behalf, when we should only have to admire and learn. The *Tale* could
certainly have sustained some deepening of her maternal anguish without
losing its character and efficacy as a 'lesson'—although, as we have seen,
mediaeval literature dealing with the Virgin and Child shows how
careful writers had to be in providing a didactic *reason* for their emo-

tional display. It is obviously dangerous for us to be too sorry for Griselda if she is to teach us to be 'constant in adversitee': our compassion must be directed and qualified, for 'happy is the man whom God correcteth'.

But the *Tale* cannot be preserved as a lesson if, in addition to this, we are instructed, even encouraged to feel human contempt for the means by which that lesson is conveyed. Griselda may pass without struggle from her one telling, critical comment upon Walter (ll. 852–7) to joyful acclamation of his loving provision for her and the children. It is not so easy for the reader, led as he has been, by an indignant narrator into a state of dissatisfaction with the conduct of the story.

The confused moral ordering of the Tale: its 'two worlds'

Basically, the trouble originates in an inability to decide upon and abide by one single set of moral standards for the *Tale*. For some of the time we move in a world which transcends ordinary value-judgements, and sees all experience, pleasure or pain, as part of a lonely journey towards perfection—'if thou wilt be perfect . . .' In this world, which is more akin to that of the saint or the mystic than to that of the 'Mother of Sorrows', the spectacle of fortitude triumphing over tremendous odds is expected to exhilarate and strengthen, rather than move to extreme compassion. Those who are called to this arduous life must welcome suffering as a means to great rewards. As we have seen from an examination of the language of the poem, Chaucer (in the guise of Clerk or narrator) is sometimes concerned that we should be able to have this kind of perspective upon events: there are moments when the grave declarations of Griselda, the 'special', allusive settings of speech or action ask us to consider that 'the situation is only in part perceptual'. The sight of Griselda

> . . . ay sad and constant as a wal,
> Continuynge evere hire innocence overal (1047–8)

can inspire a sober pleasure in the onlookers; the greater solemnity and splendour of the feast of reconciliation compared with the earlier marriage feast does seem symbolic of the spiritual 'costage' required and obtained satisfactorily of Griselda (ll. 1125–7).

But, as so much of the poem tells us—and in so lively, pointed, and characteristically Chaucerian manner—the moral standards appropriate to ordinary human behaviour powerfully influence the poet's attitudes and procedures. In a world of ideal values, Griselda's trial is something to rejoice over: the severity of Walter, even the *evil* of Walter could be seen as desirable, since they prove, once and for all, the indestructible nature of her faith.[1] The story of Job, in which Satan is allowed by God to smite Job, and show ultimately, that he is 'a perfect and an upright man', illustrates this point. Walter's words to her

> 'I have thy feith and thy benyngnytee,
> As wel as evere womman was, assayed,
> In greet estaat, and povreliche arrayed.
> Now knowe I, dere wyf, thy stedfastnesse . . . '(1053-6)

could have been made totally acceptable.

In a world of actuality, however, Griselda's sufferings become pitiable, and Walter's machinations abominable. Viewed as a human document, the *Tale* is cruel, unnatural and unconvincing, and it is just this 'human view' which is irresistible to Chaucer, and which urges him to dramatise and *then* criticise what he has created.

We are, then, very much 'between two worlds'; both are capable of inspiring fine poetry in contrasting styles—the one expressing itself in austere modes, with controlled religious echoes, the other in lively language, critical, sentimental, dramatic. But they are virtually irreconcilable—at least, within the limits of this *Tale*, and it is interesting that Chaucer does not seem to recognise the problem he sets himself and his readers by attempting to juxtapose, rather than to relate, both perspectives upon the narrative.

The Clerk's epilogue: satire and idealism

Outside the limits of the *Tale*, he allows the Clerk to make full recognition of the difference between high idealism, and common practice. The moral conclusion

> Lat us thanne live in vertuous suffraunce. (1162)

is followed by a passage which comments briskly upon the practical impossibility of finding 'in al a toun Grisildis thre or two . . .' If, during the *Tale*, we have sometimes been uncertain about the exact identity of the narrator, we are now clearly intended to understand that the voice we hear is that of the Clerk, speaking familiarly to his fellow-pilgrims, and establishing a second *raison d'être* for his story—an outer frame of

---

[1] See, for instance, the simpler and more 'satisfactory' presentation of human suffering in the *Man of Law's Tale*.

reference. We are invited to see it as part of a debate on the nature and conduct of the marriage relationship—a debate which has been making progress from the *Miller's Tale* onwards, and which the *Merchant's* and *Franklin's Tales* will bring to such opposed conclusions. When the Clerk pays suspiciously cheerful homage to the Wife of Bath, '. . . whos lyf and al hir secte God mayntene' | *In heigh maistrye, and elles were it scathe . . .*' (ll. 1171–2), a number of points come to mind: the Wife's indignation about the 'clerkly' attitude to women and marriage, for instance—

> 'For trusteth wel, it is an impossible
> That any clerk wol speke good of wyves,
> But if it be of hooly seintes lyves,
> Ne of noon oother womman never the mo . . .
> *(Wife of Bath's Prologue*, ll. 688–691)

and the scorching conclusion to her 'exemplary' *Tale*:

> 'And eek I praye Jhesu shorte hir lyves
> That wol nat be governed by hir wyves . . .
> *(Wife of Bath's Tale*, 1261–2)

It is the Clerk's triumph that he has produced a story of a virtuous wife, near enough to 'hooly seintes lyves', certainly, but sufficiently distinguished from them to make any protest difficult for the Wife of Bath. And his story was concerned with the rewards of feminine submission. This dramatic crossing of theories and personalities puts us firmly in a more circumscribed and easily defined milieu. The change-over is clearly marked by the style—after

> Lat us thanne lyve in vertuous suffraunce.

comes a different sort of phrasing and tone—

> . . . But o word, lordynges, herkneth er I go:

This passage from the hopeful spirituality of the original epilogue, composed by Petrarch near to the end of his life in the house set high among the Euganean hills, to what looks at first like tolerant scepticism—

> I wol with lusty herte, fressh, and grene,
> Seyn yow a song to glade yow, I wene;
> And lat us stynte of ernestful matere. (1173–5)

is a skilfully managed return to the miscellaneous crowd of pilgrims on the road to Canterbury. The humorous, deprecating words of the Clerk seem to be admitting what the poem itself struggled to resist: the impossibility of discovering and presenting such high and lonely qualities in terms of real flesh and blood. It was the dramatist's feeling for the 'alloy' in the gold of human nature which led to the questioning and modification of an austere religious lesson; the Clerk gives a nostalgic turn to the line, but it has a direct relevance to what has been happening in the poem:

> . . . if that they were put to such assayes,
> The gold of hem hath now so badde alayes
> With bras, that thogh the coyne be fair at ye,
> It wolde rather breste a-two than plye. (1166–9)

For we remember that although the heroine *is* preserved as an object of pure admiration, she comes very near to 'breaking-point': the metal bends dangerously on the one occasion when she accuses Walter of seeming kindness only (ll. 852 foll.).

The final reconciliation

This second summing-up, then, in the person of the Clerk, appears a first to be accommodating his story to the vision of the pilgrims with stronger concessions to the variety and fallibility of ordinary life than Petrarch's conclusion was willing to allow. Comfortable, if slightly regretful, common-sense appears to be his theme. But, as the 'song' develops, his purposes show themselves more seriously. The taking of a common-sense view (such as the Wife of Bath, with her reliance upon 'experience' would have approved) and the exaggeration of it until it becomes entirely ludicrous and grotesque are, in fact, ways of defending the basic premises of the Griselda story. Realism is pressed so far that idealism begins to seem desirable—even accessible. Weighted imagery '—syn ye be strong as is a greet camaille . . .', '. . . beth egre as is a tygre yond in Ynde . . .', '. . . ay clappeth as a mille . . .', '. . . the arwes of thy crabbed eloquence | Shal perce his brest . . .' (ll. 1196, 1199, 1200, 1203–4), familiar vocabulary ('prudence, humylitee, innocence, reverence') used in unfamiliar, unpleasant context—

> O noble wyves, ful of heigh *prudence*,
> Lat noon *humylitee* youre tonge naille . . .
> Beth nat bidaffed for youre *innocence*,

But sharply taak on yow the governaille ...
... Ne dreed hem nat, doth hem no *reverence* ...
(1183-4, 1191-2, 1201)

are designed, of course, to release the laughter which the *Tale* has firmly suppressed: they are also designed to recommend, tacitly, those very virtues and behaviour they seem to scorn. If the companionable reference to the Wife of Bath gave pilgrims and readers any sense of relief, of relaxation, the Clerk's 'finale' shows them how false it was. This mockery, in which he is so eloquent, achieves what the *Tale* itself, with its confused ordering of values, could not do: it makes 'Grisildis, pacient and kinde' a more acceptable, less preposterous creation than the Wife of Bath and 'archewyves' of her kind.

E

4. Summing-up: Chaucer's poetic methods and intentions

What impresses the reader, first and last, about the *Knight's* and *Clerk's Tales* is the variety, both of style and attitude, which Chaucer provides within such relatively limited art-forms—the chivalric romance and the moral tale. Neither poem takes in large areas of human experience, large areas of the social scene. As they were received by Chaucer, in their original state, they were certainly more anxious to exclude certain elements from their vision than to widen it, and with all the changes he made, Chaucer preserved a good deal of this 'exclusiveness' of form and vision. The outer shape of the poems is conventional: by their own definition, they are still concerned to speak of 'royal linage and richesse', and of 'sharpe scourges of adversitee' in language which more often describes the rituals of secular and religious life than the accidents, the casual disorder of human existence.

But variousness there is, in spite of this. Neither of his famous con-temporaries, William Langland or the *Gawain* poet, can rival Chaucer for the near-virtuosity of his stylistic range. The *Knight's Tale* mingles formal lament and address, offhand comment, dramatic exchange, sumptuous description and philosophic statement with no hint of self-conscious display. Even in richest poetic modes, Chaucer gives no im-pression of indulgence—an accusation which *can* sometimes be levelled at the alliterative writers of the fourteenth century. The *Clerk's Tale*, in fact, shows that he can use vocabulary quite as barely and functionally as Langland, in *Piers Plowman*, harnessing his poetic strength for religious purposes. In the same work, however, and with the same lack of self-consciousness, dramatic, intimate, and sentimental styles are given a part to play, and contribute to the total effect and meaning of the poem. When we consider not only the range of language but the range of approach to subject matter—by turns reverent, serious, admiring, sceptical, indignant, facetious and sorrowful—we might once more, even for these two *Tales* alone, endorse Dryden's comment:

> . . . 'Tis sufficient to say according to the Proverb, that here is God's Plenty.[1]

[1] *Preface* to *Fables Ancient and Modern*, ed. J. Kinsley, *The Poems and Fables of John Dryden* (O.U.P., 1962), p. 531.

But it would not be sufficient, if we wish to do Chaucer justice. He is a far more interesting and, in many senses, more difficult poet than those words suggest. When, in the same essay, Dryden notices that Chaucer 'writes not always of a piece; but sometimes mingles trivial Things with those of greater Moment' (ibid., p. 533), he draws attention to something which is one of the main virtues of Chaucer's work and, at the same time, one of its most puzzling characteristics. The reverse side of this variety, this 'plenty', can be a changeableness, an inconstancy of purpose and attitude which sometimes endangers the total unity, and the total power of a creative work.

Variousness and inconsistency of procedure

In his serious poems, if not in those of slighter intent, Chaucer is often a curiously erratic artist. Able to build up to superb dramatic climaxes, he is liable to follow them with comment unsuitable, even banal. Having carefully channelled his poetry towards a particular effect, he can sacrifice all he has done for a momentary triumph of a quite contrary sort. He may give the reader misleading expectations of a scene, and he may sum up an episode or a complete poem in a way which seems to ignore his chosen method of presentation. The *Knight's* and the *Clerk's Tales* give frequent examples of this kind of enigmatic procedure. Within a single speech, he can shift position and style so rapidly that we may be persuaded of a quite illusory logic or consistency: the speech of Theseus in the *Knight's Tale* and the last twenty stanzas of *Troilus and Criseyde* are of this order.

Such willingness to preface or to confirm with contrasting material and in a contrasting tone *can* be put to excellent artistic purposes—the rich ironies of *Troilus and Criseyde*, for instance, in which the idealism of Troilus constantly clashes against the humorous, sometimes indecent worldliness of Pandarus: the brilliant mock-heroic exercise of the *Nun's Priest's Tale*, the extravaganza of the *Tale of Sir Thopas*. But it can equally well confuse artistic and philosophic issues. It is difficult to know, sometimes, exactly what accounts for Chaucer's sudden abandonment of our attentive sympathy, his apparent contracting-out of a situation—especially since it can occur at a key point in the progress of a poem.

The mediaeval and modern reader: different conditions and criteria

This feeling of 'abandonment' is probably far more acute for the modern than for the mediaeval reader. *Hearing* a work more often than *reading* it on the manuscript page, Chaucer's audience would naturally feel less critical towards switches of attitude and expression. The episodic nature of a poem, its inconsistencies and its contradictions would not be so apparent in oral delivery. When we attempt to justify or explain away some of the discrepancies in *Troilus and Criseyde*, we should remember Chaucer's own words:

> Go, litel bok, go, litel myn tragedye, . . .
> And red wherso thow be, or elles songe . . . (1786, 1797)

and the manuscript painting of him, reading it aloud to the Court.[1] And if the actual conditions of delivery did not encourage a mediaeval poet to be anxious about consistency on all levels of his composition, neither did the accepted literary theory of his day. The rhetorical text-books, which influenced Chaucer so strongly in matters of poetic procedure and ornament,[2] are not concerned with total unity of form. The problem of organising a large work means, for them, the selection of one out of several accredited methods of beginning and ending, the suiting of style to material, and the ingenious amplification of theme by all kinds of decorative devices. If a poet was not naturally endowed with an ability to shape and discipline his art, he could not have learnt how to do so from the available 'artes poeticae'.

Moreover, it has already been pointed out, with perfect relevance to Chaucer's poetry, that the aesthetic of the age, the aesthetic of Gothic art, favoured episodic composition:

> Gothic art leads the onlooker from one detail to another and causes him . . . to 'unravel' the successive parts of the work, one after the other.[3]

All these factors may well explain why Chaucer does not hesitate to change attitude and style in the interests, perhaps, of a wealthy and varied rather than a consistent work of art. If 'local richness' rather than 'global unity' was acceptable to the period in tapestry and painting, why not

---

[1] Reproduced from Corpus Christi College, Cambridge, MS. 61, f. 1b, in *M.L.R.*, XLIV (1949), Plate facing p. 161.

[2] For an analysis of an 'ars poetica' which is known to have been used by Chaucer, see J. W. H. Atkins, *English Literary Criticism: the Mediaeval Phase* (Cambridge, 1943), Appendix.

[3] Quoted by Muscatine, *Chaucer and the French Tradition*, p. 168.

in poetry too? Viewed in this way, the lingering, pathetic presentation of Griselda and the angry treatment of the Marquis add to the poem's interest even if, at the same time, they increase the difficulty of a total interpretation. The heightening of the unprovoked malice of the deities in the *Knight's Tale*, the bitter complaint, the flippancies, and the philosophic 'explanations' are all to be received in turn 'like a panoramic survey, not a one-sided, unified presentation, dominated by a single point of view' (ibid., p. 167).

This reconstruction of a mediaeval view-point asks a good deal of the modern reader: it demands a suspension of critical principles widely accepted since the end of the mediaeval period. And while we may be willing to make the necessary adjustments for a tapestry or for a linear-type painting—their visual unfamiliarity is sufficiently strong and immediate to force us to some decisive action—it is not quite so easy to persuade ourselves and others to justify Chaucer's work in this way.

Chaucer's 'destructive' imaginative energy

The difficulty lies partly in the nature of the appeal that Chaucer's poetry makes to a modern reader. Unlike Dante or Langland, whose imaginations were kindled most fiercely by religious convictions and ideals, Chaucer was most deeply moved and inspired by the human scene. It is his imaginative participation in the love of Troilus and Criseyde which produces writing of warmth and excellence unique in the literature of the whole period, not his faithfulness to Christian teaching on 'this wrecched world' and 'the pleyn felicite | That is in hevene above . . .' It is his full realisation of the human predicament in both the *Knight's* and the *Clerk's Tale* which distances these poems so far from their various mediaeval sources. But Chaucer's imagination, working at full strength, often acts as a centrifugal rather than a centripetal force in his poetry. His instinctive and penetrating sympathy with the condition of man, particularly when it is in greatest stress—of pleasure or pain—urges him to give it fullest creative attention, regardless of how this affects the continuity, the compactness of the total work. So, the older literary forms he uses may seem, sometimes, to be under considerable strain because of an inner destructive force: they can barely accommodate the amount of new material Chaucer wishes to introduce. On the other hand, we have seen that he seldom wishes to so re-order this material as to change entirely, to do away with the traditional shapes and attitudes his age provides for him. In the *Clerk's Tale* and the *Knight's Tale*, in

Troilus and, indeed, in the whole of the *Canterbury Tales*, we see acceptance side by side with innovation: new voices speak powerfully to us—dramatically, emotionally—as well as old.

Historical reconstruction and contemporary taste: the balance

But if, by coincidence, these new elements appeal more strongly to the modern reader, start out of the poetry with a greater poignancy and imaginative truth, we should not conclude that the mediaeval reader nor, indeed, Chaucer himself, saw the artistic graph of a poem in this way. Chaucer's very willingness to revert to pattern, to preface or to follow his creative audacities by comment of a conventional, sometimes trivial nature, to juxtapose contrasting materials and attitudes in what appears to us as artistic suicide, tends to show that the process we have been discussing is half-unconscious. There is no reason to suppose that Chaucer rated more highly parts of the *Knight's Tale* in which, to our way of thinking, his imagination functions with an unusual energy and richness. His assumption, in the *Knight's Tale*, that we will find the positioning and internal logic of Theseus's speech an entirely acceptable sequel to the dark imaginings', the sharp questionings he has already put before us, is indicative. So also is his assumption, in the *Clerk's Tale*, that we can forget the dramatic re-working of the story, the resentment, indignation, compassion he has so skilfully evoked, and make the necessary religious application.

We should not superimpose our own readings and interpretations upon his: clearly, acquiescence, the act of conformity to whatever is traditional and established, was an essential and quite natural part of Chaucer's make-up. Though there may be artistic faultiness, there is no insincerity in the endings of the two poems we have been considering, as there is none in the epilogue to *Troilus and Criseyde*, and none in the sober closing-down of that Canterbury Pilgrimage which began so exuberantly. We must, to some extent, accept the situation as a historical fact, and adapt ourselves to welcome this panorama of styles and attitudes —above all avoiding the temptation to place Chaucer 'out of his age', as a revolutionary, a malcontent, a dramatic artist advanced beyond the literary modes of his time. But we cannot be blamed if we still find that there are times when he writes about human beings as few other mediaeval poets did, with a freedom and understanding which reaches our sympathies at the highest imaginative level.

Select Bibliography

EDITIONS

F. N. Robinson, *The Complete Works of Geoffrey Chaucer* (Cambridge, Mass., 1961).

J. A. W. Bennett, *Chaucer. The Knight's Tale* (London, 1958) 2nd ed.

A. C. Spearing, *The Knight's Tale* (C.U.P., 1966).

K. Sisam, *The Clerkes Tale of Oxenford* (Oxford, 1923).

CRITICAL COMMENT UPON THE TALES

W. Frost, 'An Interpretation of Chaucer's *Knight's Tale*', *R.E.S.*, XXV (1949), pp. 289–304.

D. Everett, *Essays on Middle English Literature* (Oxford, 1955), pp. 166–9.

C. Muscatine, *Chaucer and the French Tradition* (University of California Press, 1957), pp. 175–97.

J. Sledd, 'The *Clerk's Tale*: the Monsters and the Critics', *M.P.*, LI (1953), pp. 73–82.

J. Speirs, *Chaucer the Maker* (London, 1951), pp. 121–6, 151–5.

E. T. Donaldson, *Chaucer's Poetry* (New York, 1958), pp. 901–5.

GENERAL STUDIES

E. Auerbach, *Mimesis*, tr. W. R. Trask (Princeton University Press, 1953), Ch. X.

D. S. Brewer, *Chaucer* (London, 1960), 2nd ed.

D. S. Brewer, *Chaucer in his Time* (London, 1963).

W. C. Curry, *Chaucer and the Medieval Sciences* (London, 1960), 2nd ed.

E. T. Donaldson, 'Chaucer the Pilgrim', *P.M.L.A.*, LXIX (1954), pp. 928–36.

J. Huizinga, *The Waning of the Middle Ages* (London, 1948).

C. S. Lewis, *The Allegory of Love* (Oxford, 1958), 3rd ed.

J. Seznec, *The Survival of the Pagan Gods* (New York, 1961), 2nd ed.

STUDIES IN ENGLISH LITERATURE No. 5

General Editor

David Daiches

Dean of the School of English and American Studies
University of Sussex